KV-676-298

# Contents

| | | |
|---|---|---|
| **Introduction** | | 4 |
| 1. | **Birthdays** | 6 |
| 2. | **What's in a Name?** | 21 |
| 3. | **Choosing a Name** | 33 |
| 4. | **Love and Attraction** | 55 |
| 5. | **Key to the Door** | 80 |

# INTRODUCTION

Numerology – the study of numbers – is an ancient science. There are no records of when and how it came into being but we can be fairly confident that numbers have probably been studied by just about every civilization since the beginning of time. We know from historical records that Numerology was practised by the ancient Chinese, the Egyptians, the Hebrews, the Greeks, the Arabians and the Romans. Pythogoras was one of its greatest exponents and it is from his theories and teachings, handed down from pupil to pupil, that we have been able to gain much of our understanding of the subject today.

Perhaps what Pythagoras, and sometime after him Agrippa, has taught us is that numbers can be looked at on a variety of levels, some fairly simple and others intricately complex. On the one hand there is the purely logical and linear mathematical calculation – the adding and substracting as in schoolroom sums. On the other, there is the more esoteric element to numbers, that side of the study that describes time and space and the very essence of nature itself.

It is almost as if the ancients recognised a primal mathematical formula in all matter and form, a geometric pattern that influences and governs all living things. Thus, it was believed that numbers provided the key to the mysteries of the universe. And so it was that number systems over the centuries were developed to crack the code and, slowly, as Numerology evolved into a complex language of its own, it became recognised and firmly established both for divinatory purposes and as a means of character analysis.

Essentially, Numerology is based on the principle that numbers correspond to particular forces in Nature. Each number, it is believed, emits a pulse, a vibration that

FAMILY MATTERS ✓

# THE
# SECRET POWER
# OF NUMBERS

**LORI REID**

WARD LOCK

*For*
*Victoria de Zanche*
*Destiny Path 8*

ALSO BY LORI REID IN THE
FAMILY MATTERS SERIES:
**PALMISTRY**

**A WARD LOCK BOOK**

First published in the UK 1992
by Ward Lock (a Cassell imprint)
Villiers House 41/47 Strand
LONDON WC2N 5JE

Copyright © 1992 Ward Lock

Distributed in the United States
by Sterling Publishing Co., Inc.
387 Park Avenue South, New York, NY 10016-8810

Distributed in Australia
by Capricorn Link (Australia) Pty Ltd
P.O. Box 665, Lane Cove, NSW 2066

**British Library Cataloguing in Publication Data**
Reid, Lori
   The Secret Power of Numbers. – (Family matters)
   1. Numerology
   I. Title II. Series
   133.335

ISBN 0–7063–6950–5

Typeset by Columns Design and Production Services Ltd, Reading
Printed and bound in Great Britain by Harper Collins, Glasgow

resonates differently to every other number, each one producing a particular numerical magnetism. It is this innate vibration that works on all matter, setting up patterns of co-relationships, of causes and effects. By understanding these patterns we, too, can get a glimpse of how to crack the code.

Thus times and dates, being number calculations, all hold an esoteric significance which not only have an integral meaning of their own but also interconnect and correspond to times, events, people and places in the present, in the past and in the future too. In just the same way, by giving letters of the alphabet a numerical equivalent, it is possible to convert any name into a number which then gives us an understanding of its quintessential character, meaning and significance.

Depending on the different levels of interpretation, Numerology can be as easy or as complex as the practitioner might want to make it, yet every level yields no less a fascinating picture and understanding of our universe as any other. Simply put, the system is based on the use of the nine primary numbers, each of which symbolises a basic set of principles. Each number, then, describes a group of archetypal features and paints a picture in shorthand form of the fundamental forces that underline existence. The number 2, for example, represents the passive, feminine, subordinate aspects of Nature whilst the number 8 symbolises wealth and good fortune and the number 9 describes humanitarianism, spirituality and the higher idealistic aspirations.

By using Numerology, then, our names, our dates of birth, even the number of the house in which we live will reveal a new meaning, a new understanding of the forces of Nature which permeate and govern our lives.

# Chapter 1

# Birthdays

Consider how often in the course of your daily life you have to write your date of birth. Filling in job application forms, a driving licence, starting a bank account, applying for life insurance, passport or credit cards, at the doctor's and the dentist's – in fact on practically every official document you can think of. And yet, as you blithely write down those figures, so special and so personal to you, little do you realise the significance and potency that lies within them.

Indeed, numerologists say that your destiny, and all those funny little quirks of fate that occur in your life, are linked to the very numbers that make up your date of birth.

The fundamental principle behind numerology is that every number contains a unique vibrational influence which has a direct effect on matter and on all living things. So your date of birth, then, will give a great deal of information about your life – your drives, your motivation, your expectations, your dreams and ambitions, how you work and what makes you tick.

Additionally, numbers occur in cycles and, just to send your mind in a spin for a minute, they often occur in cycles within cycles! But the critical importance about your actual date of birth is that this number will reveal insights into your life cycle and into the sequences of events that are likely to occur to you through your life.

You will already have noticed that there have been periods in your life of hectic activity followed by periods of comparative peace and quiet. There will have been times when you were brimming with inspiration and good ideas. At other times your mind might have seemed quite stagnant and life itself may have appeared dull and uneventful. Lucky opportunities perhaps have come your way with amazing regularity and then misfortune may have struck repeated blows so that you felt, for a time, that your very footsteps were dogged by bad luck.

You may also have noticed that certain numbers tend to recur in your life. Consider why you have a lucky number at all and then ask yourself how you realised that that particular number *was* lucky for you in the first place. Perhaps originally it was the winning number of a raffle ticket that you bought by chance. It won once, so next time you asked for that number again. And if it wins a second time for you, you know you're on to a good thing.

Perhaps it is that you've noticed that events turn out favourably for you on a certain date, so when that comes round you put your best efforts into it, ask for a rise, arrange a job interview or important meetings, sign agreements or target a new project to start on that very day. And when these things are more or less successful, they reinforce the notion that that is indeed an especially lucky date for you and one in which, in the future, you should project your best efforts. Similarly, you will come to realise that there are certain dates in which you are best advised to keep a low profile, for here fortune is not on your side and the vibrational influences are not in your favour.

With a little knowledge of the principles behind numerology you will be able to get a good idea of how numbers influence your life and how you are governed by the numerical cycle that is at the fundamental core of existence. And by understanding that, you will be able to turn to your advantage those numbers which are favourable to you. It all begins with your date of birth.

## DESTINY NUMBERS

When added together and reduced to a single digit, your date of birth will reveal what numerology calls your Life or Destiny Number. This number, you will find, is the one that rules your life and the one which has a habit of cropping up time and again for you with uncanny regularity.

At this level, only the primary numbers of 1 to 9 are used so that all birthdays have to be reduced to a single digit. So, to convert your date of birth you simply add together the day, month and year on which you were born. The months are converted into their numerical equivalent according to their sequence in the year so that January is 1, February is 2, March is 3, and so on to December which, of course, is 12.

Having added them together you will undoubtedly arrive at a four figure number. Now, because you will be working on the 1–9 system, this large figure has to be further reduced until a primary number is arrived at, so here you just add each digit of that compound number together, and if this produces another double figure, add those two together, and so on until you are left with a single unit. In fact, by continual addition every number, no matter how large, can be reduced to one single primary number. So, let's take as an example someone who was born on the 15th of February 1946:

## Example

| | | |
|---|---|---|
| Day | | 15 |
| Month: February = 2 | | 2 |
| Year | | 1946 |
| | Total | 1963 |

| | |
|---|---|
| Now reduce 1963 to a single digit thus: | 1+9+6+3 = 19 |
| reduce further: | 1+9 = 10 |
| still further: | 1+0 = *1* |

So the numerical value, or Destiny Number, of being born on the 15th of February 1946 is 1.

When you have converted your date of birth check below the qualities that are associated with your own personal Destiny Number. This will be the number of greatest significance in your life and the one you will find likely to recur. But make a note, too, of the numbers that vibrate harmoniously with it because these will have a positive relationship with your own Destiny Number and so are likely to be favourable to you as well.

  The Key Words for each Destiny Number will give you a brief outline of your positive characteristics and the Negative Qualities will show you the areas that perhaps could do with improvement. Also listed are the

Health Aspects that are associated with that number, together with other influences such as Colour and the day of the week that is lucky for you. But equally important information at this stage is about achieving your potential in life according to your personal number and this is contained in the section headed 'Directions'.

## DESTINY NUMBER 1

**Key words:** – will-power, purpose, daring, single-mindedness, aggression, courage, love.

**Significance:** – number 1 is a positive number. Being the first digit, it conveys a sense of creativity and originality.

**Negative Qualities:** – arrogance is the major pitfall of this number. Because it has the connotation of single-mindedness, 1 can become egocentric, selfishly blind to the needs of others, self-centred and inconsiderate in its pursuit of its own independence and race to become the first, the biggest and the best.

**Directions:** – it is either through physical activity, such as in sports, or through the active use of creative ideas that those with a 1 Destiny Number will succeed in life.

**Health aspects:** – relates to the head and lungs.

**Colour association:** – red.

**Vibrates with:** – 1, 4 and 7.

**Avoid:** – 6.

**Planetary influence:** – Sun.

**Lucky day:** – Sunday.

# DESTINY NUMBER 2

**Key words:** – balance, co-operation, constructivity, considerateness, placidity, receptivity.

**Significance:** – the number 2 is both positive and negative. It is the number of opposites, of contrast, of duality. It is a passive number, always coming down on the side of justice, striving to attain harmony and balance in life.

**Negative Qualities:** – the dual nature of the number can produce a lack of self-confidence and thus lead to indicision and a good deal of 'sitting on the fence'. The negative side of 2, therefore, symbolises a refusal to accept responsibility and an inability to make positive decisions.

**Directions:** – best achievements for 2 Destiny Numbers come through team work and work involving co-operation with others.

**Health aspects:** – relates to the brain, the solar plexus and the nervous system.

**Colour association:** – orange.

**Vibrates with:** – 2, 7, 8 and 4.

**Avoid:** – 5.

**Planetary influence:** – Moon.

**Lucky day:** – Monday.

## DESTINY NUMBER 3

**Key words:** – energy, self-expression, intellect, wit, persuasive charm, success, versatility.

**Significance:** – 3 is the sign of the Trinity and symbolised by the triangle. Psychologically, it represents sociability and the healing professions. Its forte lies in diversification of interests and the connection with people and the public at large.

**Negative Qualities:** – jealousy, superficiality and impatience are the major down-falls of the number 3. It is a changeable, mutable number, with so many strings to its bow that it can become inconstant, scattering its energies and depleting its resources.

**Directions:** – success may be achieved by 3 Destiny Numbers through their heightened creative talents in conjunction with their excellent social skills.

**Health aspects:** – number 3 corresponds to language so will relate to the organs of speech which include the tongue, the throat and voice-box.

**Colour association:** – yellow.

**Vibrates with:** – 3, 6 and 9.

**Avoid:** – 4 and 8.

**Planteary influence:** – Jupiter.

**Lucky day:** – Thursday.

# DESTINY NUMBER 4

**Key words:** – practicality, self-control, steadfastness, conscientiousness, faithfulness.

**Significance:** – 4 is the sign of the square and, as such, it is a solid, stable number. In nature it is seen to recur in the 4 seasons, the 4 elements of Earth, Air, Fire and Water, in the 4 points of the compass. Thus, a sense of order and routine is associated with 4. Psychologically, it is the number of the builder, of practical construction, dependable and hard-working, solid as a rock.

**Negative Qualities:** – the solid stability and steadfastness of this number can turn into a negative, stubborn, plodding, dyed-in-the-wool attitude to life.

**Directions:** – steady work which prides itself on its thoroughness and good, solid common-sense is the way 4 Destiny Numbers will climb the ladder to success.

**Health aspects:** – relates to the stomach.

**Colour association:** – green.

**Vibrates with:** – 4, 1, 7 and 8.

**Avoid:** – 5.

**Planetary influence:** – Uranus.

**Lucky day:** – Sunday.

# DESTINY NUMBER 5

**Key words:** – adventure, aspiration, freedom, belief, change, versatility, sensuality, sexuality, lasciviousness.

**Significance:** – 5 is the number of the pentangle, the five-pointed star believed to possess magical powers and thus used as a mystical symbol. It is associated with gregariousness, adaptability and versatility and is the mark of the quick-witted thinker. It is highly appropriate that 5 is the number of the senses because more than anything else this digit is associated with self-indulgence. It is the number that rules the physical pleasures in life: eating, drinking, having sex. Indeed, all to do with fertility and procreation is linked with the number 5.

**Negative Qualities:** – the negative side of the number 5 is selfishness, instability, irresponsibilty, over-indulgence and a lack of self-discipline. The sensuality associated with this digit can all too easily turn into licentiousness and, in extreme cases, into deprativity.

**Directions:** – for the 5 Destiny Number success may come through entrepreneurial projects and schemes. Those who are less business-minded may find that life as a traveller/explorer fulfills their every satisfaction in life.

**Health aspects:** – 5 relates to the liver and the gall bladder.

**Colour association:** – blue.

**Vibrates with:** – 5 and 3.

**Avoid:** – 4.

**Planetary influence:** – Mercury.

**Lucky day:** – Wednesday.

# DESTINY NUMBER 6

**Key words:** – responsibility, dependability, integration, family-orientation, kindness, sympathy, service to others.

**Significance:** – 6 is the hexagon and also the inter-twined equilateral triangles that form the Jewish symbol known as the Star of David. It is a homely number, representing domesticity, reliability and responsibility. It is the number associated with healing and with the welfare of the nation. Idealism, honesty and harmony are the principles governing the number 6.

**Negative Qualities:** – obstinacy is perhaps the most negative quality. Other minus factors are a sense of over-protection and an instinct to meddle in other people's affairs.

**Directions:** – 6 Destiny Numbers often succeed in vocational work. People with this number have the potential to achieve a high degree of respect from their colleagues and could well climb to a lofty position in the community. The phrase 'A Pillar of Society' fits this number well.

**Health Aspects:** – 6 relates to the circulatory system, to the heart and the blood stream.

**Colour association:** – indigo.

**Vibrates with:** – 6, 3 and 9.

**Avoid:** – 1 and 8.

**Planetary influence:** – Venus.

**Lucky day:** – Friday.

# DESTINY NUMBER 7

**Key words:** – mystery, introspection, intellect, sensitivity, philosophy, discernment, solitariness.

**Significance:** – throughout history the number 7 has had a mystical significance for a wide range of cultures and religions because it is regarded as a complete or perfect number divisible by no other numbers except itself and 1. Beginning with Biblical times we have the period of Creation performed within the seven days of the week, there are the seven gifts of the Holy Ghost, the seven-branched candlestick, or menorah, that represents the presence of God in the Jewish temple, the seven notes that form the music of the spheres, the Seven Stars or Pleiades and the Seven Wonders of the World. As a vibratory number, 7 is associated with wisdom and the intellectual pursuit of knowledge. There is a strong discerning element to this number, which demands perfection. It rules selectivity so that quality is prized above quantity. Sophisticated, cultured and refined, number 7 is imbued with a mystical spiritual outlook and takes a lofty view of life.

**Negative Qualities:** – secretiveness and an almost morbid liking for solitude. Its lofty view can turn into condescention and sarcasm levelled at anything or anyone considered to be inferior.

**Directions:** – intellectual thought, philosophy and scientific research are the fields which will bring success and achievement to 7 Destiny Numbers. Delving into the realm of the occult, complementary studies or New Age subjects could also bring honours to these people.

**Health aspects:** – 7 relates to the spleen.

**Colour association:** – violet.

**Vibrates with:** – 7, 1, 2 and 4.

**Avoid:** – 9.

**Planetary influence:** – Neptune.

**Lucky day:** – Monday.

## DESTINY NUMBER 8

**Key words:** – materialism, power, success, influence, understanding, practicality, organizational flair, ambition.

**Significance:** – Oriental philosophy considers the number 8 as the luckiest number of all. Indeed, symbolically it is associated with materialism and worldly success. Cool and calculative in outlook, 8 is the number of big business, of commerce, of ambition, of executives in their pursuit for material prosperity.

**Negative Qualities:** – these lie in the unscrupulous pursuit of ambition. It is the drive for recognition and material gain that gives this number its negative image of impatience, intolerance, of bossiness and insensitivity.

**Directions:** – straight-forward honesty in business dealings is paramount for 8 Destiny Numbers if they wish to gain health, wealth and success in life. They seem to be naturally born with the Midas touch but Machiavellian tactics, dishonesty and underhandedness are for them the quickest way to fall into disfavour and into financial ruin.

**Health aspects:** – 8 rules the eyes and the lower intestines.

**Colour association:** – milky-white.

**Vibrates with:** – 8, 2 and 4.

**Avoid:** – 3 and 6.

**Planetary influence:** – Saturn.

**Lucky day:** – Saturday.

## DESTINY NUMBER 9

**Key words:** – humanitarianism, philanthropy, compassion, understanding, idealism, romance.

**Significance:** – number 9 is associated with high principles. It is the number of the philosopher, high-minded and broad-thinking. Idealistic and romantic, it governs all manner of humanitarian concerns. Sympathy, empathy and good-will towards one's fellow man come under the asupices of the number 9.

**Negative Qualities:** – 'Jack of all trades and master of none' may well be applied to the number 9. Impulsiveness, lack of self-discipline and a tendency to become distracted, to lose concentration all too easily are drawbacks here.

**Directions:** – philanthropic gestures and humanitarian pursuits are more likely to see the money flow out rather than flow in. But material prosperity is not essentially what makes 9 Destiny Numbers happy and fulfilled individuals. Success for them, then, is more likely to stem from the satisfaction they derive from the service they give to others and from the good cheer they spread to mankind.

**Health aspects:** – this number rules the sexual organs and the urinary system.

**Colour association:** – crimson.

**Vibrates with:** – 9, 3 and 6.

**Avoid:** – 7.

**Planetary influence:** – Mars.

**Lucky day:** – Tuesday.

Now that you have calculated your Destiny Number and have built up a profile of yourself and of your potential in life you can start to use the Power of Numbers to your advantage. Experiment by scheduling important appointments on favourable days. If you are a 6, for example, choose the 6th day of the month in which to begin a new project or on which to sign an agreement. Or at least a day which adds up to 6 – the 15th or the 24th, let's say. And perhaps your best efforts or new plans could be put into operation in June, which is the 6th month of the year.

As an exercise, write out a list of important events that have occurred to you beginning with your date of birth. Against each entry remember to convert the dates into a primary number. The sort of events to jot down might include the date of a change of residence, when you left school, started a job, went to college, received promotion, married, had a baby, the death of a parent, winning a large sum of money, emigrated. Now look at the dates when these important events occurred and see if any of them, or the Destiny Numbers, or even the interval of years between these big events, recur.

Many famous people throughout history have discovered the power of their Destiny Numbers and used them to their advantage. Amongst them is the much-cited businessman W. K. Kellogg whose Destiny Number was 7. He insisted on signing all important documents on the 7th of the month and finalising all deals either in July, the 7th month, or on a day whose numbers reduced to 7. Either because of his shrewd business mind, or because of his clever manipulations with his Destiny Number, or both, W. K Kellogg built up an empire worth millions.

So, having worked out the numerical equivalent of your date of birth, which is unchangeable, go on to the next chapter and work out your Expression Number. If the two vibrate harmoniously together, there is every chance of success in life. If they are discordant, perhaps it is possible to change its vibrational influence, shorten your name, use a nick-name or even change it altogether and then stand back and see how that can change the whole course of your life!

# Chapter 2

# WHAT'S IN A NAME?

The name you were given at birth is more than a mere label which distinguishes you from the next person. Your name reveals a great deal about you. It can give clues about your nationality, ancestry, status and position. It can reveal your parent's tastes, inclinations, political persuasions, with a few exceptions it denotes your gender and, because fashions for names vary from generation to generation, it can also hint your age. In fact, before you even enter the room, your name has already painted an image picture of you in other people's minds.

Whether in the flesh you can actually live up to that image, either physically or psychologically, is a very interesting matter and gives rise to several questions. For example, is it pure luck or chance that a certain name suits a certain individual? Is it that we grow to 'fit' our names, as it were? Or is it perhaps to do with other people's expectations, with their personal preferences, or with their direct experiences in matching characters to particular names?

Personally, I have an image picture of 'Dolores' – a voluptuous, raven-haired, Spanish beauty – complete with Latin temperament! Meeting a pale, shy, fair-skinned 'Dolores', jarred my credibility of her and shattered all my illusions. And the fact that she was flat-chested only helped to compound the disappointment. Similarly, a close friend of mine has an aversion to the name 'Agnes' because she associates it with the 'Agnes' she knew as a child who had several unsavoury personal habits, amongst which included a constantly runny nose which she would wipe on the cuff of her school shirt.

That we attribute particular characteristics to each name may also stem from the sound of the actual name itself. Some have a brittle, tough or aggressive ring to them – Rod, Rory, Crystal, whilst others are soft and sibilant – Beth, Cecil, Noah, Sophia. This can be put down to the hidden vibrational influence a name gives out. According to numerology, each letter of the alphabet has a numerical equivalent and, as such, every word may be converted into a number in just the same way that a date of birth is reduced to a single digit.

Just as the date of birth produces a Destiny Number, so the conversion of a name into its numerical value produces what is known as an Expression Number. Each Expression Number has a specific meaning and will give valuable insights into character and personality.

# EXPRESSION NUMBERS

To convert your name into its Expression Number is a simple process using the Alphabet Conversion Chart:

## LETTER CONVERSION CHART

| 1 | 2 | 3 | 4 | 5 | 6 | 7 | 8 | 9 |
|---|---|---|---|---|---|---|---|---|
| A | B | C | D | E | F | G | H | I |
| J | K | L | M | N | O | P | Q | R |
| S | T | U | V | W | X | Y | Z |   |

Take all your names that were given to you at birth, each with its exact spelling, and convert each letter into its numerical equivalent. Add all the numbers together and then keep adding until you have reduced the number to a single digit.

### *Example*

| S A R A H | E L I Z A B E T H | J O N E S |
|---|---|---|
| 1+1+9+1+8 | 5+3+9+8+1+2+5+2+8 | 1+6+5+5+1 |
| = 2+0 | = 4+3 | = 1+8 |
| = 2 | = 7 | = 9 |

Total   $2 + 7 + 9 = 1 + 8 = 9$

Thus, the Expression Number for the name Sarah

Elizabeth Jones is 9. So, the characteristics associated with the Number 9 are those which Sarah projects to the outside world. The concepts behind 9 encapsulate her image, her persona, how she comes across to other people.

Once you have established your own Expression Number you can find out how people see you and the sort of character you present by referring to the Personality Profile for your special number in the next section.

But supposing you don't like that character sketch? Supposing you don't like your name at all and have wanted all your life to change it? Supposing, for professional reasons, you are advised to change your name completely? What then?

Indeed, unlike your date of birth which is unchangeable, it IS possible to change your name and, of course, people do for all sorts of reasons. Names are shortened, nick-names become established, surnames may change with marriage, writers may use pseudonyms, singers and actors, especially, often use stage names that are totally different to their own.

Changing your name, then, may indeed have an impact on your character and personality. Simply dropping, or perhaps adding, a middle name, for example, could change the numerical value and thus produce a completely different Expression Number. Sarah Elizabeth Jones which, as was calculated, reduces to a 9, becomes a 2 (20 + 18 = 38 = 11 = 2) when the middle name is dropped. And if she's always been known as Sally, which is a recognised derivative of Sarah, her Expression Number becomes 6 (Sally = 15 = 6, Jones = 18 = 9, 6 + 9 = 15 = 6).

What, one wonders, might have become of Madonna or Bob Dylan if they had kept their original names – would Madonna (Expression Number 8) have been such a huge international star if she had remained Louise

Ciccone (Expression Number 7)? And would Bob Dylan (Expression Number 3) have been plucked out of obscurity to voice with his music the protest of a whole generation if he had retained his original name, Robert Zimmerman (Expression Number 1)?

For Louise Ciccone to have chosen Madonna for her stage name was a stroke of genius as its numerical value is the symbol of material prosperity and wealth. Multi-million dollar Madonna would indeed seem to be the living proof of all that the number 8 stands for. And for Robert Zimmerman, the numerical equivalent of his adopted name is 3, a number which is so often associated with success in the world of music.

Incidentally, another popular singer whose adopted name also converts to 3 is Lulu. It is interesting to speculate whether her real name, Marie Lawrie (Expression Number 6) would have brought her quite the same level of success.

Imponderable questions. However, if you don't like your name or if you're unhappy with your lot in life, you might like to consider a name change too. By changing your name you will begin to express a new personality which will create a different impression, and thereby attract a whole new set of reactions and circumstances to yourself. But it needn't be such a dramatic step that would require a deed poll or a new passport. Something quite simple such as a subtle change of spelling, or a new diminuitive form of your present name might suffice to alter the overall Expression Number.

However, before embarking on any changes, firstly check out your present Expression Number and if you're still dissatisfied, decide on the sort of image picture you want to project by reading through the Personality Profiles below and then work out a name for yourself that reduces to that number. Remember that you will never completely lose the underlying vibrational influence of your original name but you can certainly overlay it as we have seen in the examples of both Bob Dylan and Madonna.

Finally, don't forget to consult the Table of Harmonies at the end of the chapter to confirm that either your present or your new Expression number vibrates harmoniously with your Destiny Number. If they do, there will be an easy interchange between your character and the way you function in life. If there is any discord between the two, it might be that you will find it more difficult to achieve your ambitions and find success and fulfillment in life. In the latter case, perhaps a change of name would indeed change the whole course of your life.

## PERSONALITY PROFILES

### EXPRESSION NUMBER 1

1 is the number of independence and self-assertiveness. There is no mistaking these individuals for they possess powerful and dominant personalities and make an impact upon all those they meet.

Strong-willed, self-sufficient, channelled and direct, these people are born leaders. They are ambitious, happier at the top than at the bottom, at the front where the action is, than bringing up the rear. Usually bright and intellligent, there is a strong element of originality and creativity in their make-up. Action is their key-word, either physical or intellectual, and those with an Expression Number of 1 will be constantly on the go, filling their lives with a whirlwind of activity.

Their greatest faults lie in their egocentric preoccupation with themselves, which can lead to inconsiderate behaviour towards others, to arrogance and to a desire to dominate and take over people and situations.

## EXPRESSION NUMBER 2

Whereas 1s are happier leading the cavalry charge, people with the Expression Number 2 prefer to be part of the support net-work, patiently waiting with the food and bandages until their assistance is required. Passive and receptive, these people possess an abundance of sympathy and understanding which makes them valuable partners and team-mates. Indeed, they are never happy alone for they prefer living and working with others, quietly dispensing the wisdom and experience they have acquired over years of sitting in the shadows and simply watching the human condition. In general shy and retiring, they are never ones to push themselves forward but are always prepared to co-operate and be carried along by the enthusiasm of others. Gentle, sensitive and intuitive, these people always seek balance and harmony in their lives.

Their faults include excessive sensitivity, indeciveness and a tendency to be over-dependant on others. Because they try so hard to avoid all forms of confrontation they invariably end up sitting on the fence.

## EXPRESSION NUMBER 3

Chatty, noisy, full of life, full of fun, the Number 3 describes a happy, lively, gregarious individual. Those who possess this as their Expression Number are bright and friendly extroverts. Ever optimistic, enthusiastic and appreciative of the joys and beauty that surround them, they spread colour and cheer wherever they go. Self-expression is the key to understanding their personalities and such people will naturally gravitate towards the Arts for they have highly imaginative and original ideas. These people are extremely talented and have no equals when it comes to creative and artistic flair, consequently Expression Number 3s will be found in the world of music, of art and, particularly, in the media. The Number 3 is an especially lucky number to possess.

Faults with Expression Number 3 lie mainly in a too frivolous or superficial attitude to life.

## EXPRESSION NUMBER 4

Number 4 represents solidity and stability. Those who possess this as their Expression Number are honest, hard working, responsible individuals, staunchly ploughing through the day, following a set routine with dogged persistence. When it comes to manual dexterity and practical skills, these people are unbeatable. Meticulous over detail, practical, level-headed and down-to-earth, they are often accused of lacking imagination and originality, so they are at their best in the fields in which they can make full use of their immense common-sense and logical mentality. Strongly authoritarian and firm believers in law and order, in the Establishment and in the 'status quo', they make upright citizens. Work-wise they may be found in traditional institutions such as in the police-force, the legal system, armed services, in banking and the Civil Service. It is by dint of their persistence and determination that Expression Number 4s are rewarded and eventually find success.

Faults with this group lie mainly in too strict an attitude to life, too stiff an upper lip so that they repress emotion, and in a too dully and plodding existance that lacks colour and variety in their daily routines.

## EXPRESSION NUMBER 5

Versatile, adaptable and restless sums up those with an Expression Number 5. Above all else, these individuals are quick-witted. They possess bright, Mercurial mentalities that pick up new skills, new information and new tricks at a mere glance. Because they are such fast learners, almost inspirational in their up-take, they can become easily bored, requiring masses of variety and distractions to keep their interest from flagging. Their razor-sharp minds, too, become impatient, especially with punctilious detail, red-tape and with crass stupidity. With their chamaeleon-like characters, people with this Expression Number are changeable and therefore perhaps unreliable, often turning out to be the mavericks in the pack. And the search for constant distraction applies equally to their need for different activities as well as different people to stimulate them both physically and mentally. Indeed stimulation is a word that applies strongly to these individuals who have a heightened libidinal drive. Amongst the Mercurial occupations that so often attract this group, sales and marketing seem to be the most popular because they not only provide the diversity that is required but also create the stimulus in which such butterfly minds can excel.

Faults attributed to this group include irresponsibility, over-indulgence and a mis-use of the senses. A Macchiavellian urge to manipulate people and situations may also be a negative tendency.

## EXPRESSION NUMBER 6

The true home-maker is symbolised by the Expression Number 6. These people are emotionally stable types and, like the 4s, tend to be solid and responsible individuals. They are family-oriented, lovers of hearth and home. Fairly creative they admire gracious living and actively seek to create a pleasing and harmonious environment wherever they are, whether this is in the home or in the workplace. Kind and understanding, those whose names convert to the Expression Number 6 make excellent partners and, especially, excellent and caring parents. They have a strong sense of service and so will be found in all areas of the vocational and caring professions.

Negative characteristics involve jealousy and, because these people often feel strongly that they know best, they do have a tendency of giving people the benefit of their advice – whether they have been invited to do so or not!

## EXPRESSION NUMBER 7

Those who belong to the Expression Number 7 group have enquiring minds. Fairly introspective types, they delight in quietly taking things apart in order to see how they work. This applies not only to inanimate objects but also to complex abstract principles, to psychological concepts and established belief systems. These people actively seek peace and quiet in which they can persue their analytical trains of thought and, as such, prefer to work on their own rather than with others. Generally highly intelligent, they make excellent researchers, analysts, philosophers and scientists and may be found in the many intellectual professions and fields of endeavour. As individuals, however, these people may be somewhat cool and aloof in their approach to others and, because they don't readily open up or express their innermost feelings, they can all too easily be misunderstood.

Pitfalls include secretiveness and a tendency to repress emotion.

## EXPRESSION NUMBER 8

People who fall into this group are highly achievement-motivated, prepared to work day and night in order to amass their fortune and secure material prosperity. Excellent organisers and confident of their powers and abilities, they persue their goal relentlessly and often ruthlessly too. The attainment of financial security seems to be uppermost in their minds and they will brook little opposition or interference along the way. These are the executives, the bankers, financiers, managers, the wheeler-dealers, the men and women who control the purse-strings of the economy. Wherever big business is taking place, there will be Number 8s tightly holding the reins. Status, too, is important to them because this is the external manifestation of their wealth. So, grand financial schemes, commercial expertise, money, power, position and as many of the material comforts that wealth will buy, just about sums up the motivating principles underlying this Expression Number.

Negative aspects include a lack of sensitivity and an uncontrollable lust for power.

## EXPRESSION NUMBER 9

The Expression Number 9 describes those with a strong altruistic and philanthropic streak to their nature. Unlike 8s, whose efforts tend to be self-centred, 9s are true humanitarians who make it their life ambition to further the cause of humanity and to better the lot of mankind. Theirs is a broad, universal outlook, never insular nor parochial, they seek as wide a range of experience as life has to offer them. Busy, active people, they rush about cramming as much as they can into their day, though perhaps it is a characteristic of this group that they don't always achieve the sort of success their efforts deserve. But success can be attained, and often reward comes to them through their imaginative and creative endeavours. 9 people are both spiritual and intellectual with a strong tendency towards idealism. Charismatic individuals, they have the power to influence others and to fire them with their own brand of enthusiasm and optimism. Consequently, they make excellent teachers, imparting their understanding and experiences with wisdom and compassion.

Faults applicable to this group include impatience – they can seriously champ at the bit and become extremely frustrated and even bitter if restricted or if they feel their efforts have not been suitably recognised or rewarded.

## TABLE OF HARMONIES

| Expression Number | Harmonious | Dissonant |
|---|---|---|
| 1 | 1, 4, 7 | 6 |
| 2 | 2, 4, 7, 8 | 5 |
| 3 | 3, 6, 9 | 4, 8 |
| 4 | 1, 4, 7, 8 | 5 |
| 5 | 3, 5, | 4 |
| 6 | 3, 6, 9 | 1, 8 |
| 7 | 1, 2, 4, 7 | 9 |
| 8 | 2, 4, 8 | 3, 6 |
| 9 | 3, 6, 9 | 7 |

# Chapter 3

# CHOOSING A NAME

Choosing the name for a new baby can be one of the most enjoyable preoccupations of parenthood. On the other hand, it can also be one of the most frustrating and disconcerting experiences that confront a young mother- or father-to-be.

To begin with, the choice of Christian name must please both parents – something that can lead to a bone of contention in the family for several months before the birth. Then, it must blend happily with the surname. Stevie Smith has a nice ring to it, but try getting your teeth around Christabel Alison Bracegirdle, for example. And then what if, as inevitably will happen, that pretty name, so lovingly and carefully chosen, should be reduced to an absurd nickname or, worst still, to one which can be held up to ridicule? A close relative of mine decided to call her son Adam in the belief that it was impossible to shorten the name any further and was horrified some years later to hear his schoolfriends calling him Ad! And wasn't it interesting to note that the Prince and Princess of Wales stated to the nation on the birth of their first son that his name could certainly be foreshortened but ONLY to Wils and NEVER to Willie!

Fashions have a strong hand in determining which name will go down on the birth certificate. There are many 20-year-old Waynes and Shanes, Traceys and Sharons but there aren't many Veras or Stanleys. Trends seem to go in cycles, perhaps sometimes sparked off by a famous film star or the name of a royal baby. 30 years ago you would not so readily have called your baby daughter Daisy or Rosie or Sophie. Today, look at any infant school register and names such as these which were popular in Victorian and Edwardian times are making a strong come-back. But beware, saddle a child with an obviously unfashionable name and you may well be looking at an identity crisis in some 16 or 17 years' time!

So the choice of name will reflect many things and take into account family traditions, fashions, personal likes and dislikes. But after all the considerations have been made the choice of name should not solely be left to a question of taste. Indeed, as the previous chapter shows, there is a good deal more to a name than simply how it sounds because within its hidden numerical equivalent lies the influence that shapes the character and personality of your son or daughter.

Before rushing out to register your child, then, consider carefully its numerical equivalence and ask yourself if that is the personality you would like your child to have. For example, you may decide to choose the name Cathleen for your daughter. Convert the letters and reduce them to a primary number and you will see that Cathleen equals $3+1+2+8+3+5+5+5 = 3+2 = 5$. If you like a particular name but dislike its resonant character, you could spell it a different way. Cathleen with a C adds up to 5 but what if it were spelt with a K as in Kathleen. Here the name reduces to $2+1+2+8+3+5+5+5 = 3+1 = 4$. But wait a minute, whichever way it is spelt, the chances are that Cathleen or Kathleen will be shortened so this possibility, too, should be taken into consideration. If the child becomes known as Cathy, the numerical equivalent will be thus – $3+1+2+8+7 = 2+1 = 3$. Alternatively, spelt with a K, the name becomes Kathy – $2+1+2+8+7 = 2+0 = 2$.

As a quick reference guide, below is a list of names with their numerical equivalents so you can see at a glance to which number each name corresponds; wherever possible, alternative spellings and the popular shortened versions of the name are also included. And just to refresh your memory here is a quick checklist of the key characteristics associated with each number.

1.  Power, dynamic energy, ambition, egotism, pride.

2.  Balance, cooperation, moderation, emotionality, instability.

3.  Intellect, creativity, originality, judgement, fault-finding.

4.  Construction, industriousness, practicality, stubbornness.

5.  Activity, energy, wit, restlessness, sexuality.

6.  Domesticity, responsibility, common-sense, service, possessiveness.

7. Knowledge, introspection, understanding, sensitivity, secretive.

8. Materialism, success, money, commerce, business, domineering.

9. Philosophy, compassion, open-mindedness, idealism, impulsiveness.

# A

| Name | Numerical Equivalent | Name | Numerical Equivalent |
|------|------|------|------|
| Abigail | 5 | Amy | 3 |
| Abbey | 8 | Andrea | 7 |
| Adele | 9 | Angela | 4 |
| Alessandra | 4 | Ann | 2 |
| Alexandra | 8 | Anna | 3 |
| Alexis | 7 | Anne | 7 |
| Alice | 3 | Antonia | 2 |
| Alison | 7 | Audrey | 2 |
| Amber | 3 | Avril | 8 |
| | | | |
| Adam | 1 | Andrew | 2 |
| Adrian | 2 | Andy | 8 |
| Alasdair | 2 | Angus | 8 |
| Alastair | 9 | Anthony | 7 |
| Alister | 3 | Tony | 2 |
| Alexander | 3 | Arthur | 5 |
| Alec | 3 | Aubrey | 9 |
| Alex | 6 | Austin | 3 |
| Sandy | 9 | | |

# B

| Name | Numerical Equivalent | Name | Numerical Equivalent |
|---|---|---|---|
| Barbara | 7 | Beverly | 8 |
| Beatrice | 9 | Bianca | 3 |
| Beatrix | 7 | Bonny | 5 |
| Belina | 2 | Brenda | 8 |
| Bernadette | 4 | Bridget | 2 |
| Beth | 8 | Bryony | 9 |
| | | | |
| Barry | 1 | Bob | 1 |
| Benedict | 8 | Bobby | 1 |
| Ben | 3 | Bradley | 4 |
| Benjamin | 5 | Brendan | 4 |
| Bill | 8 | Brian | 8 |
| Billy | 6 | Bruce | 4 |
| Blake | 4 | Bruno | 7 |

# C

| Name | Numerical Equivalent | Name | Numerical Equivalent |
|---|---|---|---|
| Camilla | 6 | Chris | 3 |
| Candy | 2 | Chrissie | 9 |
| Cara | 5 | Christy | 3 |
| Carla | 8 | Chrystal | 7 |
| Carly | 5 | Crystal | 8 |
| Carmel | 7 | Claire | 3 |
| Carol | 4 | Clara | 8 |
| Caroline | 5 | Clare | 3 |
| Carrie | 9 | Clarissa | 1 |
| Cassandra | 8 | Claudia | 6 |
| Catherine | 2 | Cleo | 8 |
| Cath | 5 | Colette | 8 |

| | | | |
|---|---|---|---|
| Cathy | 3 | Colleen | 3 |
| Catriona | 9 | Cora | 1 |
| Celia | 3 | Coral | 4 |
| Charlotte | 3 | Cordelia | 4 |
| Cheryl | 8 | Corinna | 2 |
| Chloe | 7 | Corinne | 6 |
| Christina | 2 | Cressida | 6 |
| Christine | 6 | Cynthia | 8 |
| | | | |
| Cameron | 6 | Cliff | 9 |
| Campbell | 1 | Clifford | 1 |
| Carl | 7 | Clive | 6 |
| Cary | 2 | Colin | 8 |
| Casey | 8 | Colan | 9 |
| Chad | 7 | Connor | 7 |
| Charles | 3 | Conor | 2 |
| Charlie | 2 | Conrad | 1 |
| Chas | 4 | Corey | 3 |
| Chuck | 1 | Cory | 7 |
| Carlo | 4 | Courtney | 4 |
| Carlos | 5 | Craig | 2 |
| Christian | 2 | Crispin | 7 |
| Christopher | 4 | Curtis | 9 |
| Chris | 3 | Cyril | 4 |
| Clay | 5 | | |

# D

| Name | Numerical Equivalent | Name | Numerical Equivalent |
|---|---|---|---|
| Daisy | 4 | Diana | 2 |
| Dana | 2 | Diane | 6 |
| Danielle | 8 | Dilys | 6 |
| Daphne | 3 | Donna | 3 |
| Dawn | 6 | Dolly | 5 |
| Deborah | 8 | Doreen | 7 |

| | | | |
|---|---|---|---|
| Debbie | 9 | Dorothea | 5 |
| Deidre | 9 | Dorothy | 6 |
| Delia | 4 | Dot | 3 |
| Denise | 2 | Dulcie | 9 |
| Desiree | 2 | | |
| | | | |
| Dale | 4 | Desmond | 2 |
| Damian | 6 | Des | 1 |
| Damien | 1 | Dominick | 6 |
| Damon | 2 | Donald | 5 |
| Dan | 1 | Don | 6 |
| Daniel | 9 | Donal | 1 |
| Darius | 9 | Dougal | 6 |
| Dave | 5 | Douglas | 7 |
| David | 4 | Doug | 2 |
| Dean | 6 | Drew | 5 |
| Denis | 6 | Duncan | 3 |
| Denzil | 7 | Dustin | 6 |
| Derek | 7 | Dylan | 2 |
| Derik | 2 | Dwayne | 9 |
| Dirk | 6 | | |

# E

| Name | Numerical Equivalent | Name | Numerical Equivalent |
|---|---|---|---|
| Edith | 1 | Emilia | 4 |
| Edna | 6 | Emily | 1 |
| Edwina | 1 | Emma | 5 |
| Eileen | 5 | Emmeline | 4 |
| Elaine | 1 | Erica | 9 |
| Eleanor | 7 | Estella | 2 |
| Elinor | 1 | Estelle | 6 |
| Elizabeth | 7 | Esther | 3 |
| Eliza | 8 | Eugenia | 8 |

| Name | Numerical Equivalent | Name | Numerical Equivalent |
|---|---|---|---|
| Liz | 2 | Eugenie | 3 |
| Lizzie | 6 | Eva | 1 |
| Ellen | 3 | Eve | 5 |
| Eloise | 2 | Evelyn | 2 |
| Elsbeth | 8 | | |
| Eamon | 3 | Emil | 3 |
| Edgar | 8 | Emile | 8 |
| Edmund | 7 | Emlyn | 6 |
| Edward | 1 | Errol | 5 |
| Ed | 9 | Ethan | 3 |
| Eddie | 9 | Eugene | 3 |
| Edwin | 1 | Gene | 4 |
| Eli | 8 | Evan | 6 |
| Eliot | 7 | Everett | 5 |
| Elliot | 1 | Ewan | 7 |
| Ellis | 3 | Ewen | 2 |
| Elton | 3 | Ewart | 4 |
| Elvis | 4 | Ewert | 8 |
| Elwyn | 7 | | |

# F

| Name | Numerical Equivalent | Name | Numerical Equivalent |
|---|---|---|---|
| Faith | 8 | Fleur | 8 |
| Fay | 5 | Flora | 7 |
| Faye | 1 | Florence | 6 |
| Felicity | 8 | Frances | 3 |
| Fenella | 1 | Frankie | 1 |
| Fern | 7 | Francesca | 7 |
| Fiona | 9 | Freya | 1 |
| | | | |
| Fabian | 6 | Foster | 2 |
| Fairfax | 2 | Francis | 7 |
| Farley | 4 | Franklin | 4 |
| Felix | 2 | Frederick | 7 |

| Fergus | 4 | Fred | 6 |
| Finn | 7 | Freddie | 6 |
| Floyd | 8 | | |

# G

| Name | Numerical Equivalent | Name | Numerical Equivalent |
| --- | --- | --- | --- |
| Gabrielle | 8 | Ginette | 8 |
| Gail | 2 | Giselle | 6 |
| Gayle | 5 | Glenda | 7 |
| Gemma | 3 | Glennis | 8 |
| Genevieve | 4 | Glynis | 5 |
| Georgia | 8 | Gloria | 8 |
| Giorgiana | 5 | Golda | 3 |
| Georgina | 4 | Goldie | 7 |
| Georgette | 3 | Grace | 7 |
| Geraldine | 3 | Gracie | 7 |
| Gerry | 1 | Greta | 6 |
| Gerda | 8 | Gretchen | 8 |
| Germaine | 9 | Gretel | 4 |
| Gilda | 6 | Gwen | 4 |
| Gillian | 1 | Gwenda | 9 |
| Gill | 4 | Gwendolen | 9 |
| Gina | 4 | Gwendoline | 9 |
| | | | |
| Gabriel | 9 | Giles | 7 |
| Gareth | 5 | Glenn | 7 |
| Garth | 9 | Glyn | 4 |
| Garry | 6 | Gordon | 1 |
| Gaston | 4 | Graham | 3 |
| Gavin | 8 | Graeme | 4 |
| Geoffrey | 6 | Grant | 6 |
| Geoff | 5 | Gregory | 5 |
| Jeffrey | 3 | Greg | 1 |
| Jeff | 9 | Gregg | 8 |

| | | | |
|---|---|---|---|
| George | 3 | Gunter | 4 |
| Gerald | 2 | Guy | 8 |
| Gerry | 1 | Gwyn | 6 |
| Jerry | 4 | | |

# H

| Name | Numerical Equivalent | Name | Numerical Equivalent |
|---|---|---|---|
| Hana | 6 | Helga | 6 |
| Hannah | 1 | Henrietta | 1 |
| Harriet | 7 | Henrie | 5 |
| Hattie | 9 | Henrika | 3 |
| Hayley | 4 | Hermione | 6 |
| Hazel | 7 | Hester | 3 |
| Heather | 2 | Hilary | 1 |
| Heidi | 8 | Holly | 9 |
| Helen | 8 | Hope | 8 |
| Helena | 9 | Hyacinth | 7 |
| | | | |
| Hamish | 4 | Bertie | 5 |
| Harley | 6 | Herb | 6 |
| Harold | 4 | Herman | 5 |
| Harry | 7 | Hiram | 4 |
| Harvey | 7 | Howard | 6 |
| Henry | 7 | Hugh | 8 |
| Herbert | 4 | Hugo | 6 |
| Bert | 9 | Hywel | 1 |

# I

| Name | Numerical Equivalent | Name | Numerical Equivalent |
|---|---|---|---|
| Imogen | 9 | Iris | 1 |
| Ines | 2 | Isabel | 3 |

| Inez | 9 | Isabella | 7 |
| Ingrid | 7 | Isobel | 8 |
| Irene | 6 | Belle | 9 |
| Rene | 6 | Bella | 5 |
| Renie | 6 | Ivy | 2 |
| | | | |
| Ian | 6 | Isaac | 6 |
| Iain | 6 | Isaiah | 2 |
| Igor | 4 | Ivan | 1 |
| Ira | 1 | Ivor | 1 |
| Irving | 7 | Ifor | 3 |

# J

| Name | Numerical Equivalent | Name | Numerical Equivalent |
| --- | --- | --- | --- |
| Jacqueline | 7 | Jill | 7 |
| Jackie | 3 | Jillia | 8 |
| Jacky | 5 | Jilly | 5 |
| Jade | 2 | Gillian | 1 |
| Jamie | 2 | Joan | 4 |
| Jane | 3 | Joanna | 1 |
| Jayne | 1 | Johanna | 9 |
| Janie | 3 | Jocelyn | 3 |
| Janine | 8 | Josse | 5 |
| Janet | 5 | Josephine | 2 |
| Janice | 6 | Jo | 7 |
| Jasmin | 3 | Josie | 4 |
| Jasmine | 8 | Joy | 5 |
| Jean | 3 | Joyce | 4 |
| Jeanne | 4 | Judith | 9 |
| Jeannie | 4 | Judy | 6 |
| Jemima | 6 | Jodie | 7 |
| Jennifer | 9 | Jodi | 2 |
| Jennie | 3 | Julia | 8 |
| Jenny | 5 | Julie | 3 |

| Name | Numerical Equivalent | Name | Numerical Equivalent |
|------|------|------|------|
| Jessica | 3 | Juliet | 5 |
| Jess | 8 | June | 5 |
| Jessie | 4 | | |
| | | | |
| Jack | 7 | Johnny | 5 |
| Jacob | 4 | Jon | 3 |
| Jake | 9 | Jock | 3 |
| James | 3 | Jonathan | 2 |
| Jamie | 2 | Jonty | 3 |
| Jim | 5 | Jordan | 8 |
| Jimmy | 7 | Joseph | 1 |
| Jason | 5 | Joe | 3 |
| Jasper | 6 | Joey | 1 |
| Jay | 9 | Joshua | 2 |
| Jed | 1 | Josh | 7 |
| Jeremy | 4 | Jude | 4 |
| Jerry | 4 | Julian | 4 |
| Joel | 6 | Justin | 3 |
| John | 2 | | |

# K

| Name | Numerical Equivalent | Name | Numerical Equivalent |
|------|------|------|------|
| Karen | 4 | Kaye | 6 |
| Kate | 1 | Keeley | 9 |
| Katie | 1 | Kelly | 2 |
| Katharine | 6 | Kerry | 5 |
| Katherine | 1 | Kerrie | 3 |
| Katrina | 2 | Kim | 6 |
| Kitty | 4 | Kimberley | 1 |
| Kathleen | 4 | Kirsten | 6 |
| Kathy | 2 | Kirsty | 3 |
| Kay | 1 | Kylie | 8 |
| | | | |
| Kane | 4 | Kenny | 6 |

| | | | |
|---|---|---|---|
| Karl | 6 | Kent | 5 |
| Kegan | 2 | Kevin | 7 |
| Keith | 8 | Kieran | 4 |
| Kelvin | 1 | Kirk | 4 |
| Kenneth | 5 | Kit | 4 |
| Ken | 3 | Kyle | 8 |

# L

| Name | Numerical Equivalent | Name | Numerical Equivalent |
|---|---|---|---|
| Lara | 5 | Lita | 6 |
| Laura | 8 | Lois | 1 |
| Lauren | 8 | Lola | 4 |
| Laurel | 6 | Lolita | 6 |
| Laurie | 3 | Loris | 1 |
| Lori | 9 | Lorna | 6 |
| Lavender | 9 | Lorraien | 2 |
| Leah | 8 | Louisa | 5 |
| Leanne | 6 | Louise | 9 |
| Leigh | 5 | Lulu | 3 |
| Leila | 3 | Loveday | 3 |
| Leonie | 6 | Lucia | 1 |
| Lesley | 6 | Lucy | 7 |
| Lillian | 6 | Lucille | 2 |
| Lily | 4 | Lucinda | 1 |
| Linda | 4 | Lydia | 6 |
| Lindsay | 3 | Lyn | 6 |
| Lyndsay | 1 | Lynn | 2 |
| Lisa | 5 | Lynne | 7 |
| Lise | 9 | Lynette | 2 |
| Lisette | 9 | | |
| | | | |
| Lachlan | 6 | Lewis | 5 |
| Laird | 8 | Louis | 4 |
| Laurence | 7 | Llewellyn | 3 |

| | | | |
|---|---|---|---|
| Lawrence | 9 | Lloyd | 5 |
| Larry | 2 | Luke | 4 |
| Laurie | 3 | Luther | 3 |
| Lee | 4 | Lyle | 9 |
| Lennie | 5 | Lyn | 6 |
| Leo | 5 | | |

# M

| Name | Numerical Equivalent | Name | Numerical Equivalent |
|---|---|---|---|
| Madeleine | 5 | Martine | 8 |
| Magdalen | 3 | Mary | 3 |
| Maddie | 9 | Maria | 6 |
| Magda | 8 | Marie | 1 |
| Madonna | 8 | May | 3 |
| Donna | 3 | Maureen | 5 |
| Mandy | 3 | Mavis | 1 |
| Marcelle | 6 | Maxine | 3 |
| Marcia | 9 | Melanie | 5 |
| Margaret | 2 | Melinda | 4 |
| Maggie | 6 | Melissa | 6 |
| Mae | 1 | Melody | 2 |
| Margarita | 7 | Melodie | 9 |
| Marguerite | 9 | Meryl | 1 |
| Meg | 7 | Michaela | 7 |
| Megan | 4 | Michelle | 4 |
| Margot | 2 | Millicent | 7 |
| Marianne | 3 | Millie | 6 |
| Marilyn | 2 | Milly | 8 |
| Marina | 2 | Miranda | 6 |
| Marnie | 6 | Moira | 2 |
| Marian | 2 | Molly | 5 |
| Marion | 7 | Mollie | 3 |
| Marlene | 5 | Mona | 7 |
| Marlee | 9 | Monica | 1 |

| | | | |
|---|---|---|---|
| Marsha | 6 | Morag | 9 |
| Martina | 4 | Morwenna | 4 |
| | | | |
| Magnus | 3 | Mat | 7 |
| Malcolm | 6 | Max | 2 |
| Marcus | 3 | Mel | 3 |
| Marius | 9 | Michael | 6 |
| Mario | 2 | Mick | 9 |
| Mark | 7 | Mike | 2 |
| Marc | 8 | Miles | 4 |
| Marco | 5 | Myles | 2 |
| Martin | 3 | Morgan | 5 |
| Martyn | 1 | Morris | 2 |
| Matthew | 9 | Murray | 6 |
| Matthias | 1 | | |

# N

| Name | Numerical Equivalent | Name | Numerical Equivalent |
|---|---|---|---|
| Nadine | 3 | Nickie | 6 |
| Nancy | 6 | Nicole | 4 |
| Naomi | 7 | Nina | 2 |
| Natalie | 8 | Nora | 3 |
| Natasha | 1 | Norah | 2 |
| Nicola | 9 | Noreen | 8 |
| Nicky | 8 | Norma | 7 |
| | | | |
| Nathaniel | 3 | Nick | 1 |
| Nathan | 4 | Nicky | 8 |
| Nat | 8 | Nigel | 2 |
| Neil | 4 | Noah | 2 |
| Neal | 5 | Noel | 1 |
| Niall | 3 | Norman | 3 |
| Neville | 7 | Nye | 8 |
| Nicholas | 9 | | |

# O

| Name | Numerical Equivalent | Name | Numerical Equivalent |
|---|---|---|---|
| Odette | 6 | Olwen | 6 |
| Odile | 9 | Opal | 8 |
| Olga | 8 | Ophelia | 3 |
| Olivia | 5 | Ottile | 9 |
| | | | |
| Olaf | 7 | Oswald | 2 |
| Oliver | 9 | Ozzie | 9 |
| Orlando | 7 | Otis | 9 |
| Osbert | 7 | Otto | 7 |
| Oscar | 2 | Owen | 3 |

# P

| Name | Numerical Equivalent | Name | Numerical Equivalent |
|---|---|---|---|
| Pamela | 3 | Perdita | 1 |
| Pandora | 6 | Peta | 6 |
| Patience | 1 | Petra | 6 |
| Patricia | 5 | Petula | 3 |
| Patrice | 9 | Philippa | 2 |
| Pat | 1 | Pippa | 4 |
| Patsy | 9 | Phoebe | 6 |
| Patty | 1 | Phyllis | 2 |
| Paula | 6 | Pia | 6 |
| Paulette | 1 | Polly | 8 |
| Pauline | 6 | Poppy | 7 |
| Pearl | 7 | Primrose | 6 |
| Peggy | 6 | Priscilla | 9 |
| Penelope | 7 | Prudence | 5 |
| Penny | 2 | Prunella | 9 |

| | | | |
|---|---|---|---|
| Patrick | 6 | Peter | 1 |
| Pat | 1 | Pete | 1 |
| Paddy | 5 | Philip | 7 |
| Paul | 5 | Phil | 9 |
| Percy | 4 | Pip | 5 |
| Peregrine | 7 | Piers | 4 |
| Perry | 1 | | |

# Q

| Name | Numerical Equivalent | Name | Numerical Equivalent |
|---|---|---|---|
| Queenie | 4 | | |
| Quentin | 1 | | |

# R

| Name | Numerical Equivalent | Name | Numerical Equivalent |
|---|---|---|---|
| Rachel | 2 | Roberta | 7 |
| Ramona | 8 | Roma | 2 |
| Raquel | 2 | Rosalie | 7 |
| Rebecca | 1 | Rosalind | 1 |
| Beckie | 8 | Rosamund | 6 |
| Becky | 1 | Rosa | 8 |
| Regan | 9 | Rose | 3 |
| Regina | 9 | Rosie | 3 |
| Renata | 5 | Rosanne | 5 |
| Renee | 2 | Rosemary | 6 |
| Rhea | 5 | Rowena | 4 |
| Rhoda | 1 | Roxane | 5 |
| Rhona | 2 | Ruby | 3 |
| Rhonda | 6 | Ruth | 4 |
| Rita | 3 | | |

| Name | | Name | |
|------|---|------|---|
| Ralph | 1 | Rodney | 9 |
| Ramsay | 5 | Roger | 9 |
| Randal | 5 | Roland | 1 |
| Randolph | 7 | Rolando | 7 |
| Randy | 8 | Rolf | 6 |
| Raymond | 9 | Rollo | 9 |
| Ray | 8 | Ronald | 1 |
| Reuben | 2 | Ron | 2 |
| Rex | 2 | Ronnie | 3 |
| Rhys | 7 | Rory | 4 |
| Richard | 7 | Ross | 8 |
| Richie | 7 | Roy | 4 |
| Rick | 5 | Royston | 9 |
| Dick | 9 | Rudie | 3 |
| Robert | 6 | Rufus | 4 |
| Robbie | 6 | Rupert | 8 |
| Bob | 1 | Russell | 7 |
| Bobby | 1 | Russ | 5 |
| Robin | 4 | Rusty | 4 |
| Roddie | 1 | Ryan | 4 |
| Rod | 1 | | |

# S

| Name | Numerical Equivalent | Name | Numerical Equivalent |
|------|----------------------|------|----------------------|
| Sabrina | 1 | Sherri | 5 |
| Sadie | 2 | Sherry | 2 |
| Sally | 6 | Shirley | 6 |
| Samantha | 5 | Sidonia | 8 |
| Sam | 6 | Sidonie | 2 |
| Sammy | 8 | Simone | 3 |
| Sandra | 3 | Siobhan | 5 |
| Sandie | 7 | Sonia | 4 |
| Sandy | 9 | Sonya | 2 |
| Sara | 3 | Sophia | 5 |

| Name | Numerical Equivalent | Name | Numerical Equivalent |
|------|------|------|------|
| Sarah | 2 | Sophie | 9 |
| Selina | 6 | Sophy | 2 |
| Serena | 8 | Sorrel | 6 |
| Sharon | 3 | Stella | 6 |
| Sheena | 7 | Stephanie | 7 |
| Sheila | 9 | Susan | 2 |
| Sheelagh | 2 | Susanna | 8 |
| Shelley | 5 | Susie | 1 |
| Samuel | 8 | Sinclair | 9 |
| Sam | 6 | Spencer | 8 |
| Saul | 8 | Stanley | 6 |
| Scott | 5 | Stephen | 6 |
| Sean | 3 | Steven | 4 |
| Sebastian | 9 | Stefan | 2 |
| Seth | 7 | Steve | 8 |
| Shane | 2 | Stevie | 8 |
| Sheridan | 6 | Stewart | 7 |
| Simon | 7 | Stuart | 7 |
| Si | 1 | Stu | 6 |
| Sim | 5 | | |

# T

| Name | Numerical Equivalent | Name | Numerical Equivalent |
|------|------|------|------|
| Tabitha | 7 | Tess | 9 |
| Tamara | 9 | Tessa | 1 |
| Tamsin | 4 | Thelma | 5 |
| Tamsyn | 2 | Tiffany | 9 |
| Tammy | 9 | Tilly | 6 |
| Tania | 9 | Tina | 8 |
| Tanya | 7 | Toni | 4 |
| Tansy | 7 | Topaz | 6 |
| Tara | 4 | Tracey | 9 |
| Teresa | 5 | Tracy | 4 |

| Name | Numerical Equivalent | Name | Numerical Equivalent |
|------|------|------|------|
| Theresa | 4 | Trixie | 4 |
| Terry | 5 | Trudy | 7 |
| | | | |
| Teddy | 4 | Toby | 8 |
| Terry | 5 | Todd | 7 |
| Theo | 3 | Travis | 8 |
| Thomas | 4 | Trent | 5 |
| Tom | 3 | Trevor | 8 |
| Tommy | 5 | Tristan | 2 |
| Timothy | 2 | Tristram | 1 |
| Tim | 6 | Troy | 6 |
| Tobias | 3 | | |

# U

| Name | Numerical Equivalent | Name | Numerical Equivalent |
|------|------|------|------|
| Ulrica | 1 | Unity | 8 |
| Una | 9 | Ursula | 2 |
| | | | |
| Ulric | 9 | Urian | 9 |

# V

| Name | Numerical Equivalent | Name | Numerical Equivalent |
|------|------|------|------|
| Valentina | 8 | Vicky | 7 |
| Valerie | 9 | Vickie | 5 |
| Val | 8 | Viola | 5 |
| Vanessa | 9 | Violet | 2 |
| Vera | 1 | Virginia | 8 |
| Verity | 9 | Ginnie | 4 |
| Veronica | 6 | Ginny | 6 |
| Victoria | 7 | Vivienne | 1 |

| Name | Numerical Equivalent | Name | Numerical Equivalent |
|------|------|------|------|
| Vaughan | 2 | Vince | 8 |
| Vernon | 7 | Virgil | 5 |

# W

| Name | Numerical Equivalent | Name | Numerical Equivalent |
|------|------|------|------|
| Wanda | 7 | Willow | 4 |
| Wendy | 8 | Wynne | 9 |
| Wallace | 3 | Wils | 9 |
| Wallis | 4 | Willy | 9 |
| Ward | 1 | Bill | 8 |
| Warren | 7 | Billy | 6 |
| Wayne | 5 | Winston | 6 |
| Wesley | 8 | Wyatt | 8 |
| William | 7 | Wyndham | 7 |
| Will | 2 | | |

# X

| Name | Numerical Equivalent | Name | Numerical Equivalent |
|------|------|------|------|
| Xanthe | 9 | Xenia | 8 |
| Xavier | 7 | | |

# Y

| Name | Numerical Equivalent | Name | Numerical Equivalent |
|------|------|------|------|
| Yasmine | 5 | Yvette | 7 |
| Yolanda | 9 | Yvonne | 5 |

| Yehudi | 9 | Yuri | 1 |

# Z

| Name | Numerical Equivalent | Name | Numerical Equivalent |
|------|----------------------|------|----------------------|
| Zara | 1 | Zita | 2 |
| Zelda | 3 | Zoe | 1 |
| Zenia | 1 | | |
| | | | |
| Zack | 5 | Zeke | 2 |
| Zane | 1 | Zenon | 2 |
| Zebedee | 7 | | |

# Chapter 4

# LOVE AND ATTRACTION

Numbers fall into discrete groups and the way they relate to each other depends very much on the vibration each puts out as to whether it will harmonize, attract or oppose another given number. There are three groups, each containing three numbers which radiate in a similar way and therefore complement each other. The first group belongs to the **Physical** category and contains the numbers **2, 4 and 8**. The second is known as the **Emotional** group and contains the numbers **3, 6 and 9**. And the third group is the **Mental** category containing the remaining three numbers **1**, **5** and **7**.

Numbers within the same group, then, share an overall similarity in their nature and so it is said that these numbers have a special affinity with each other. If you calculate the numerical equivalent of your name and that of your lover, which gives both your Expression numbers, you will be able to determine whether you belong to the same harmonic group and thus whether you are numerically compatible.

Some numerologists maintain that in order to work out your compatibility numbers, you have to convert the whole name that you were given at birth.

## EXAMPLE

| ELEANOR | JOANNA | GRAY |
|---|---|---|
| 5+3+5+1+5+6+5 | 1+6+1+5+4+1 | 7+9+1+7 |
| = 3+0 = 3 | = 1+8 = 9 | = 2+4 = 6 |

Total 3+9+6 = 1+8 = 9

Others, however, believe that when you are considering the question of attraction and compatibility, you should work on the name you are most familiarly known by. Eleanor Joanna Gray may indeed be on your birth certificate but if everybody knows you as Ellie Gray, the number which you are most commonly vibrating will be:-

## EXAMPLE

| ELLIE | GRAY |
|---|---|
| 5+3+3+9+5 | 7+9+1+7 |
| = 2+5 = 7 | = 2+4 = 6 |

Total 7+6 = 1+3 = 4

I tend to follow the latter school of thought because I believe that we not only automatically modify our personalities to match any variation in our names, but we also assume characteristics that are reflected back to us by other people's preconception of the character that is associated with a particular name. So, Frederick, for example, is likely to behave and to be treated very differently to Fred. Similarly, Christine is a very different type of person to Chrissy.

So, to establish the nature of the relationship that you have built up between yourself and your lover you must calculate your Expression numbers by converting your names into their numerical equivalents.

**EXAMPLE**

JULIET
1+3+3+9+5+2
= 2+3 = 5

CAPULET
3+1+7+3+3+5+2
= 2+4 = 6

Total 6+5 = 1+1 = *2*

ROMEO
9+6+4+5+6
= 3+0 = 3

MONTAGUE
4+6+5+2+1+7+3+5
= 3+3 = 6

Total 3+6 = *9*

It would be interesting to speculate, had Romeo and Juliet's tragic fate not taken place, what sort of relationship these two star-crossed lovers might have had together. Well, numerologically, Juliet's Expression number is 2 whilst Romeo's is 9. Check out below what their chances of compatibility might have been and then work out your own Expression number and that of your lover the same way and see how you two are likely to respond to one another?

Just remember in all your calculations, though, that each number is imbued with both positive and negative characteristics. We are none of us perfect, nor indeed, all bad.

## THE NUMBER ONE LOVER

People whose Expression number is ONE need love and romance (with a capital R!) in their lives. They are adventurous people and make sensual and sexy partners. But they need more than just sex in their relationships, they need a meeting of minds too, so they will be looking for intellectual stimulation from their partners as well as true love. If they can't get the intellectual buzz they may well start to look elsewhere.

More than anything, ONES hate to be pinned down. They feel stifled if they think their independence has been taken away from them so unless they can maintain a certain sense of freedom within a relationship, they may simply spread their wings and seek wider horizons.

ONES are very proud people and in any relationship they have to come out on top. They cannot bear to be criticised and, if they are, they have a tendency to stonewall you. But it is their egotism and selfishness that are perhaps their most negative characteristics in a relationship and which are most likely to upset the apple-cart.

### IN PARTNERSHIP

*1 + 1*  Though on the same wave-length, two ONES together are likely to constantly fight for supremacy.

*1 + 2*  ONES are physically attracted to TWOS and it is true that TWOS need a strong partner in life which ONES undoubtedly are. However, TWOS need cosseting, they need plenty of love and understanding and masses of togetherness and perhaps ONES' selfishness might get in the way.

*1 + 3* This is an excellent combination. ONES are mentally and emotionally attracted to THREES whose interesting and fun-loving attitude to life would provide a good complement to them.

*1 + 4* Not an especially easy partnership. ONES may perhaps find FOURS just a little too stolid for their adventurous spirits.

*1 + 5* ONES are mentally and physically attracted to FIVES. This relationship has all the makings of a potentially exciting and stimulating partnership.

*1 + 6* This combination is potentially disasterous! ONES are adventurous, SIXES are stay-at-homes, ONES have a touch of irresponsibility, SIXES have a strong sense of duty. This couple is not really on the same wave-length at all.

*1 + 7* ONES have a strong mental attraction to SEVENS. They find SEVEN's coolness and aloofness an irresistible challenge.

*1 + 8* ONES are physically attracted to EIGHTS. These two can go a long way together – especially if they're in business together.

*1 + 9* These two can form strong bonds of friendship together. Both are independent types, outgoing and prone to intense emotions. Potentially good.

# THE NUMBER TWO LOVER

People whose Expression number reduces to TWO are sensitive and understanding. Because they are passive, especially sexually, they are best in a supportive role. They actively seek a loving relationship for they need a solid, reliable partner who they can respect and who will provide, physically, emotionally and financially, a warm, stable and secure nest. In return, they make responsive lovers and offer loyalty and devotion, a sympathetic ear, a charming, tactful and adaptable nature, and a loving environment to return home to at the end of the day.

In general, they are gentle and readily respond to kindness. Given tenderness, understanding and appreciation, they visibly open up like flowers in the sun. A relationship based on teamwork and on cooperation is essential to them, for they are born to share and to please those they love. Above all else, TWOS love peace and harmony and will do their utmost to avoid quarrels or any form of discord in their domestic lives.

As they hate hurting and upsetting others they may hang on in an unhappy relationship rather than make a clean break of it. Indeed, many TWOS seem to experience more than their fair share of relationship problems, especially through the first half of their lives, perhaps because some can become easy prey and are easily taken advantage of, or perhaps it may be due to the fact that they have such idealistic expectations about their partners that they can all too easily feel let down.

## IN PARTNERSHIP

**2 + 1** TWOS are physically attracted to ONES and they would provide the warm nest for ONES to return to. They certainly benefit from the strength of character that

ONES would bring to the relationship, but would they get all the personal support they need out of the partnership?

**2 + 2** Quite honestly, these two are a bit wet together! Both are passive, responsive, indecisive types and, though on the same wave-length, really need to look to stronger types for support and protection.

**2 + 3** TWOS seem to be physically and emotionally attracted to THREES as they find them lively and fun to be with. Perhaps, though, not so good as a long-term proposition because TWOS would feel insecure and undermined by THREES' gregarious and flirtatious attitude in life.

**2 + 4** These two are mentally and physically attracted to each other. Excellent combination, excellent long-term prospects.

**2 + 5** Potentially unhappy combination. TWOS could so easily be taken advantage of by the stronger but more irresponsible side of FIVES.

**2 + 6** Bingo! Super combination, both needing the same things in life. Moreover, each is physically, mentally and emotionally attracted to the other.

**2 + 7** Though TWOS may be physically attracted to SEVENS, they simply won't get the sort of warmth out of a relationship that they need.

**2 + 8** Could work well as TWOS will give EIGHTS the loyalty, devotion and dedication of an emotionally supportive partner. In return, EIGHTS would provide the material security for the partnership.

**2 + 9**  On a physical level these two could be attracted to each other. But too many differences of opinion to guarantee long-term success: TWOS tend to be inward-looking whilst NINES look outwards, so TWOS would be too parochial for NINES who have the universe at their feet.

## THE NUMBER THREE LOVER

THREES always seem to gravitate to centre-stage for they are born extroverts and are seekers after the limelight. As partners they are lively and interesting, witty and fun-loving, infecting all those around them with their own special brand of cheerfulness and enthusiasm. Never dull, they are blessed with a marvellous sense of humour and if you're feeling low just leave it to your THREE partner to pick you up and make you laugh again.

Friendship is especially important to them for they are naturally gregarious types and if married to a number THREE you will probably find that your house is constantly filled with people coming and going. Friendship, too, is essential in their personal relationships and this has to be at the very core of any loving or sexual partnership they strike up. In particular, marriage for them has to be a true partnership in every sense of the word.

Number THREES seem to possess a certain inborn flirtatiousness, especially when they are younger, and so may find it difficult to commit themselves and settle down. They have an idealistic view about marriage and once they find a partner who is happy-go-lucky, prepared to flatter them, lavish them with love, affection and attention and, moreover, tolerate their petty foibles, they will commit themselves happily and return every bit of love they are blessed to receive.

## IN PARTNERSHIP

**3 + 1**  Good rapport between these two. Fairly well on the same wave-length, each is mentally and emotionally attracted to the other. A potentially zingy relationship.

**3 + 2**  THREES could benefit from TWOS' lavish attention but in time would feel frustrated and even held back by TWOS' passivity and need for security and stability. TWOS may well suffer from THREES' cavalier attitude in any close pesonal relationship.

**3 + 3**  A relationship full of sparkle and fun but perhaps not enough seriousness here to tackle the nitty-gritty of every-day life.

**3 + 4**  Difficult, though there would be some advantages to both parties if the relationship were handled intelligently. Solid and dependable FOURS would gain from THREES's light-heartedness in life and THREES would benefit from FOURS's stability. But with the wrong pair, it would be chalk and cheese.

**3 + 5**  Brilliant all-round partnership. Mentally challenging, physically exciting, emotionally and sexually stimulating. Full of activity, masses of variety and plenty of buzz.

**3 + 6**  Another good one! Both in harmony with each other and both mentally and physically attracted to one another. SIX happily takes care of the domestic arrangements whilst THREE contributes the sparkle to the relationship.

**3 + 7**  Not terribly recommended as a long-term proposition. Though there could be a meeting of minds, there would be precious little else coming together between these two.

*3 + 8*  This relationship has great potential, especially if they run a business together and if each respects and allows the other's talents to flourish. When the combination works, it can make a materially and financially successful team.

*3 + 9*  Good harmony should exist between these two, THREES and NINES being physically and mentally attracted to each other. On a deeply personal level, though, would NINES find THREES spiritually insensitive? And could THREES put up with NINES' constant need for humanitarian fulfillment?

## THE NUMBER FOUR LOVER

FOURS are eminently dependable and reliable. They are hard-working and eager to provide stability and security for those they love. Although not good social mixers – they find it difficult to make friends – they are, nevertheless, very affectionate towards those they love. And, because they are not gregarious, their domestic life is especially important to them, dearly loving their spouses, their children and their homes.

In marriage, FOURS make conscientious, loyal and faithful partners. Fair-minded, honest and sincere, they like to build their relationships upon the solid foundations of good, old-fashioned values. These people are born with broad shoulders, tailor-made upon which they willingly place the burdens of responsibility in life. The problem is that they do tend to work too hard, almost verging on the workaholic. They have to learn to make more space for their leisure pursuits and to enjoy some quality time with their families.

For a partner, they need a good intellectual mate, someone who will keep them mentally stimulated.

Interestingly, though they like and admire a strong character in a partner, they cannot bear to be dominated, so FOURS are likely to encounter a certain amount of conflict in their relationships because of this. Perhaps, though, the most important qualities that a partner to a FOUR should possess are cheerfulness and a ready wit. Someone, in fact, who is prepared to show their number FOUR lover the lighter side of life and remind them occasionally not to take life (in general) and themselves (in paticular) quite so seriously.

## IN PARTNERSHIP

**4 + 1** Apart from needing physical comforts in life and sharing good business sense, these two don't have very much in common.

**4 + 2** Excellent relationship with a strong mental understanding and physical attraction. FOURS provide the material security whilst TWOS bring their sensitivity and responsiveness to the partnership.

**4 + 3** Rather disparate types, although if they found a true meeting ground each would benefit enormously from the other. FOURS are conservative and industrious whilst THREES are fun-loving and flirtatious with life, so FOURS could supply the material security and THREES the interest and tonic to bring the relationship alive.

**4 + 4** A strong, solid relationship although in danger of becoming stodgy. Lots of hard work, lots of seriousness and consequently lots of material and financial success. Plodding, stolid type of relationship, with few heady heights to give colour and interest to their lives.

**4 + 5** This union is not highly tipped for long-lasting

success. FOURS need a solid, stable relationship but FIVES simply can't be pinned down.

**4 + 6** A splended combination. SIXES are the domestic home-makers and excellent parents which FOURS need as a back-up in their lives.

**4 + 7** Though potentially promising as a creative meeting of minds, SEVENS are too cool, too aloof and too untenable for solid, down-to-earth FOURS, so this is an unlikely match.

**4 + 8** Brilliant relationship right across the board with masses of mental and physical attraction. Both high achievers and there is every prospect for a successful and prosperous life together.

**4 + 9** Important differences in points of view here. FOURS are inward-looking and could find NINES' global view uncomfortable. NINES need a broad-minded partner and FOURS might prove too narrow for them.

## THE NUMBER FIVE LOVER

Clever, sharp, quick-witted, street-wise FIVES are great wanderers, adventurers and travellers. More than anything else in life, they loathe the idea of being stuck in a rut, treading the same groove from 9 to 5, day in and day out. New horizons, change, variety, always having to be one step ahead is the thrill, the charge, that FIVES need to keep them stimulated, to keep the adrenalin flowing in their veins.

And they need the same sort of adventure and excitement when it comes to matters of the heart. More than any of the other Expression numbers, FIVES are sensual creatures, prone to over-indulgence of all the physical pleasures and ruled by a very strong sex-drive. Indeed, in every FIVE there's a strong touch of the Don Juans or of the Mae Wests!

Because of their philandering natures it is highly likely that they will have a good many love affairs in their youth. And when FIVES do finally decide to settle down, it will be with someone who shares their sense of romance, who will love their children and be happy to provide a warm home for their return. Moreover, it will be to someone who will offer a challenge, provide a mental stimulus and perhaps be prepared to accept a rather modern, 'open' type of relationship. Their partners will have to learn to accommodate that restless impulse of theirs and not curtail their sense of freedom and independence and, occasionally, even turn a blind eye on FIVES' little indiscretions or sexual peccadilloes.

## IN PARTNERSHIP

**5+ 1** What an exciting, stimulating and fizzy relationship this one is! Each is mentally and physically and sexually attracted to the other. The only snag is, does either of these have time to be truly understanding and sympathetic of the other or, when the chips are down, is each too egocentric or self-absorbed to really care?

**5 + 2** Difficulties would soon show up with these two. TWOS are too clinging and demanding, and need more protection and security than FIVES are prepared to give. Additionally, FIVES could all too easily take advantage of TWOS' weaker and more passive nature.

**5 + 3** Great attraction between these two and perhaps one of the best combinations for FIVES. Masses of sexual excitement. In fact, life is just one great bowl of cherries for this relationship.

**5 + 4** Different needs, different ideas, different purpose in life. FOURS need solidity and dependability but FIVES are restless and need constant change and variety, so no real meeting of minds here at all.

**5 + 5** On the same wave-length, plenty of excitement, and a life filled with passionate highs and lows. However, each too busy doing their own thing for a truly mutually loving and receptive relationship to exist for long.

**5 + 6** If SIXES were prepared to be tolerant, accepting of FIVES' vagaries and prepared to make nice warm nests ready for FIVES' return, then the relationship could work well. In reality, though, FIVES find SIXES stifling whilst SIXES find FIVES irresponsible.

**5 + 7** In as much as SEVENS like their own company and FIVES are always out and about, it would seem that these two would make little unreasonable demands on each other. When they do come together, however, they have a great deal to say to each other. Though not the makings of a truly close and loving relationship, they can, nevertheless, enjoy a brilliantly stimulating mental rapport with each other.

**5 + 8** Good for business, making for a constructive and successful partnership. For a closer union, though, FIVES would have to show a good deal more responsibility in order to keep EIGHTS' attention, and EIGHTS would have to spend less time at work and more time with FIVES in order to keep their interest alive.

**5 + 9** Potentially good all-round. Stimulating, interesting, lively partnership. Plenty of mental and physical attraction with lots of zingy sex between these two.

# THE NUMBER SIX LOVER

Domestic and home-loving, SIXES hate to live alone. They are very affectionate, loving types for whom a happy family and close relationship are essential to their well-being. Nothing makes a SIX happier than being needed because people with this name number are born to help others, to be of service not only to their immediate families, but also to the community at large.

As partners, SIXES are thoroughly dependable, responsible, sympathetic and generous to a fault. They have a tendency to be somewhat idealistic about love and marriage, perhaps all too ready to don those rose-coloured specs and dream about roses around the cottage door. Certainly, they do have a habit of placing their loved ones on pedestals and blinding themselves to their faults.

At home they are excellent at keeping house, efficient with the housekeeping and good at all domestic activities. They are the sort who are able to somehow magically transform a house into a home – they make splendid cooks, are creatively gifted when it comes to interior decorating and are blessed with green fingers so that their gardens bloom and their house-plants prosper. Many are even able to sing beautifully and/or play a musical instrument to soothe the savage breast of their mate after a stressful day at work.

Of all the Expression numbers, SIXES generally make the best parents. With wisdom and good sense, they bring up their children in a tolerant, caring and nurturing environment, take their education in hand and are generally concerned about their welfare. But perhaps the criticism that might be levelled at these otherwise seemingly faultless parents and spouses is that they can all too often become possessive and over-protective and that many of them fall into the self-righteous trap of thinking that they always know what's best for others!

## IN PARTNERSHIP

**6 + 1** Quite a few difficulties are likely to arise between these two Expression numbers in a close relationship. SIXES need more domestic security and commitment than ONES may be prepared to offer whilst independent ONES could find SIXES overwhelmingly possessive.

**6 + 2** A brilliant combination. A very compatible union arguing well for long-term success together. Each sympathetic and responsive to the other, both pulling together with the same aims and objectives in life.

**6 + 3** A winning team. These two could go far together. Mental, physical and emotional compatibility here. SIXES are happy to provide back-up security for THREES while THREES bring home the pzzazz that adds the colour and interest to the relationship.

**6 + 4** Another winner! Together these make a solid, hard-working, caring and productive couple. They share conventional views and responsible attitudes to life.

**6 + 5** Chalk and cheese, these two. SIXES need commitment, but restless FIVES can't bear to be pinned down. What's more, SIXES are far too conservative for the devil-may-care attitude of FIVES.

**6 + 6** Similar types with similar aims in life. But what happens when each thinks they *know* what's best for the other?

**6 + 7** A disasterous combination. SIXES are too warm and clinging for cool, aloof SEVENS. SEVENS are far too impersonal for cuddly SIXES.

**6 + 8**  A very good relationship. SIXES would provide all the domestic warmth and understanding that EIGHTS need whilst they provide all the material security in which SIXES can fulfill their creative talents.

**6 + 9**  A sympathetic relationship, each partner in tune and in harmony with the other. Masses of mental mind-touch, good for business and for creative and emotional fulfillment.

## THE NUMBER SEVEN LOVER

If you are married to someone whose name number is SEVEN you will know how difficult it is to penetrate the inner sanctum of their thoughts. Indeed, SEVENS are complex personalities, reserved, sensitive and aloof. 'Still waters . . .' describes them very well and because they have a tendency to guard their thoughts, to repress emotion and generally keep themselves to themselves, they are often misunderstood. Getting SEVENS to talk about their innermost feelings is like pushing a megaton boulder up a one-in-five gradient!

As they appear cool and aloof they are difficult to get to know in the first place. Then don't expect much kissing and cuddling; billing and cooing is simply not their style.

And talking of which, style is something SEVENS have plenty of. These are the most cultured and refined of individuals and their elegance and aesthetic good taste will be reflected in their homes. Everything here will be artistic and decorative and, even if they can't afford much, there will, nevertheless be a sense of quality for they possess an exquisite eye for detail. There is never confusion or clutter in the number SEVEN'S household for these people are able to imbue their homes with a sense of order, of peace and of harmony.

Just as they are discriminating about their homes, so they are equally selective when it comes to affairs of the hearts and in general SEVENS marry well. And because they choose their future spouses so carefully, once married, they tend to remain faithful. Their partners, however, must learn to live with SEVENS' need for solitude, allow them some time to themselves in the day, time to get away from the noise and the hurly-burly of modern life, to quietly gather their thoughts together and to recharge their spiritual, mental and emotional batteries.

## IN PARTNERSHIP

**7 + 1**   There is a good mental harmony between these two as they can enjoy an intellectual charge from each other. On a platonic level, then, there is a great deal of compatibility of temperament, but in the romantic or sexual relationship SEVENS could well find ONES dominant and over-bearing and may be totally turned off by their emotional ardour.

**7 + 2**   Great deal of potential irritation between these two. SEVENS are cool and seemingly uncaring towards TWOS, who are clinging and need protection and security.

**7 + 3**   A relationship with a lot of merit though at first perhaps not quite so apparent. Lots of creative spin-off, coupled with a good deal of mental and physical attraction. Only snag might arise from THREES' gregarious-ness in comparison to SEVENS' need for solitude.

**7 + 4**   A good match. Neither superficial nor gregari-ous. FOURS would benefit from SEVENS' learning whilst SEVENS could find that FOURS are able to translate their ideas into practical reality for them.

**7 + 5** Though potentially a good amount of mind-touch, apart from a possible business partnership, there's not a lot of common ground upon which SEVENS and FIVES could build a solid close relationship. FIVES are considered far too superficial by deeper-thinking SEVENS.

**7 + 6** SIXES need a warm, domestic and secure environment in which to make their homes and nurture their offspring. Moreover, SIXES need a strong net-work of friends around to give them support. These are the very needs that would irritate SEVENS who are not at all social types nor in the least domestically inclined. This, then, is not exactly a recipe for long-term happiness.

**7 + 7** Two people in harmony with each other, sharing similar tastes and similar talents. But because both are introspective there is the danger that neither would have time to give the other attention or make the effort to discuss their innermost feelings with their partner.

**7 + 8** A difficult combination here, EIGHT being materialistic and worldly-wise whilst SEVEN is soul-seeking and withdrawn.

**7 + 9** There's a chance that this could be a workable combination. Both are independent types and would respect the other's need for spiritual fulfillment. But on a more personal basis they would have to reach a certain level of understanding if the relationship were to be viable. The reason being that SEVENS could seem a little too detached whilst NINES might be considered uncaring by their partner. However, a strong physical attraction might just be enough to bond them together.

# THE NUMBER EIGHT LOVER

EIGHTS are not exactly what you would call sentimental. Never ones for being carried away by romantic ideals, they are cold realists. When it comes to affairs of the heart they know full well that love in poverty is a recipe for disaster.

People whose names have a numerical value of EIGHT are materialists at heart. They thrive on success and on the sort of secure and comfortable life that money will provide. They are very much creatures of comfort and are prepared to work hard to get what they want out of life. Alternatively, the more mercenary EIGHTS will actively look to marry into money.

Material success and all the trimmings that go with it, status symbols, influential friends, prestigious aquaintances are all important to this Expression number and they find that they naturally gravitate towards people of the same ilk. Work-wise they are likely to be in big business or run their own company, and prospective marriage partners are often met amongst people in the same line of work. In fact, many EIGHTS work together, perhaps in a joint business venture or as partners in a family concern.

Essentially, EIGHTS need to marry someone they respect, someone strong whom they can admire and who will provide the solid foundation and material security they require. In reality, many are likely to marry and divorce several times throughout their lives and often contract marriages where there is a wide disparity in their ages. Indeed, it would appear that EIGHTS find true happiness EITHER when they marry someone much older than themselves, OR, when they marry later on in life, towards their middle age.

To give them their due, once married they do deeply love their homes and their children. They especially love animals so there are likely to be quite a few pets around in the EIGHT household.

## IN PARTNERSHIP

*8 + 1* Good potential for a materially successful relationship. Both parties are ambitious go-getters so are likely to achieve their aims in life. In a romantic relationship, though, each as bossy as the other so look out for fireworks!

*8 + 2* Very good mutually receptive relationship. EIGHTS will provide the material security and TWOS will supply the spiritual back-up and support.

*8 + 3* Good prospects for this combination, especially if they are in business together. These two seem to be physically attracted, and on all levels of interaction EIGHTS provide the executive abilities whilst THREES add the glamour, status and pzzazz that lifts and lends interest to the relationship. Good whilst it lasts but perhaps not terribly long-lived as a marital union.

*8 + 4* A super match. These two are on the same wave-length, both prepared to work hard shoulder-to-shoulder to achieve their aims and ambitions in life. The only slight snag is that this relationship, concentrating as it does on all work and no play, is in danger of becoming dull and stolid. What these two need is a touch of colour to invigorate and refresh their relationship otherwise it may well turn a little stale.

*8 + 5* Technically an interesting match especially if they are in business together where EIGHTS are the executives and FIVES front the public image. In the domestic situation, however, EIGHTS might be too engrossed in their work to give their partners the attention and personal satisfaction they need. In their turn, FIVES could be seen as too restless and flighty by their more responsible partners.

**8 + 6**  A brilliant liason. Masses of mind-touch, plenty of physical attraction, both wanting the same things out of life and both prepared to support the other in the achievement of their aims on all levels of their relationship.

**8 + 7**  Aims and ambitions so disparate between these two that this is a potential recipe for a disasterous union.

**8 + 8**  This has all the elements of a Dallas-type relationship. Together these two have the Midas touch.

**8 + 9**  There is potentially a good deal of physical attraction between these two and each could benefit from the other if they work together. But on a deeper, personal level, EIGHTS may not be broad-minded and tolerant enough for NINES' humanitarian pursuits, whilst NINES could well find their partners' materialistic attitudes somewhat offensive.

# THE NUMBER NINE LOVER

To belong to the Expression number NINE means being a part of the brotherhood of man. NINES are spiritual creatures, born with the ideal of brotherly love and with broad philosophical views on life that transcend nations and boundaries. Open-minded and tolerant, they are caring and compassionate people, big-hearted and generous to a fault.

As partners they are sympathetic and understanding, but they are independent types and will suffer if their freedom is denied them. And because they take such a wide perspective, they need a partner who is equally broad-minded and prepared to take a global view of things. Anyone insular and narrow in outlook simply will not complement a NINE personality.

Immensely loving and giving, (in fact they may be described as 'life's givers'), they gladly give themselves and all they possess to the ones they love. When it comes to matters of the heart, NINES are highly idealistic and tend to be in love with love. For them, falling in love is total, and when they do, they fall completely head over heels. They crave love and affection to such an extent that they will either meet and marry the partner of their dreams very early on in life or, suffer many unhappy experiences when young simply because they mistakenly give their hearts too readily to the wrong people and end up disappointed or taken for a ride.

Theirs is an idealistic view of life and if their partners or their homes do not match up to these ideals, then that love, despite its original intensity, will soon dissipate. The sort of home life that might be described as 'kitchen sink' is definitely not for NINES. It isn't that they require a palace or even great wealth for their happiness, it is simply that people, situations and places *must* come up to the NINES' standards of excellence and *must* match their sense of aesthetics, of goodness and of loveliness.

As parents NINES will impart these high standards to their children. Sternly disapproving of any low or underhand behaviour, they teach their youngsters morality, the value of good manners and of good breeding. NINES are especially fond of children, treating them as part of the universal brotherhood, the seeds of the future that form the links, the network, of mankind.

Moreover, they are excellent home-makers, turning their hands to almost anything. With their artistic and creative abilities they can transform a shabby environment into a comfortable, attractive and pleasing place in which to live. And because they take a global view of life, their homes will have a cosmopolitan feel, with a mixture of styles and designs, filled with artifacts and treasures, lovingly brought back from their travels around the world.

## IN PARTNERSHIP

**9 + 1** Lively and stimulating relationship. Sexy and exciting. ONES have breadth of vision and are cosmopolitan enough to respect NINES' far-reaching mentality.

**9 + 2** Fairly good on a mental level, particularly when it comes to the exchange of creative ideas. On a more intimate level, NINES may find TWOS' vision of life somewhat narrow and restricting.

**9 + 3** A brilliant match! Interesting, fun-loving, buzzing, sparkling – and sexy to boot. But in their heart of hearts there will be times when NINES find THREES' attitude just a little too superficial.

**9 + 4** As much positive as negative with this couple depending on the individuals concerned. NINES bring creative inspiration whilst FOURS add practical know-how. Together they could make a formidable team, putting ideas into reality, but there are times when stolid FOURS may lack understanding of NINES' wider panoramic view of life.

**9 + 5** A magnetic attraction between these two. A lively and exciting relationship with plenty of variety and interests to share. Perhaps FIVES are not quite as deep as NINES would like at times, but plenty of other compensations to keep the partnership alive.

**9 + 6** These two Expression numbers are harmoniously suited right across the board. A very compatible union.

**9 + 7** Not a great deal in common here to sustain a long-term relationship.

**9 + 8** Plenty going for these two if they handle it well. Good for business and for the exchange of ideas. Physical attraction between them helps. On an intimate level, EIGHTS tend to be unsentimental whilst NINES are romantic. If each can make allowances for these differences of character then there's a strong chance of success, especially if the interests are on an international level.

**9 + 9** These two are certainly on the same wavelength, sharing the same aims and objectives in life. Highly-tipped for a successful relationship and if they work together for humanitarian organizations, so much the better.

## Chapter 5

# KEY TO THE DOOR

Have you noticed how each house seems to have a specific character all of its own? Some always feel friendly and welcoming, even on a dull, rainy day. Others have a stiff, clinical feel to them, cool and indifferent as soon as you walk in so you don't know whether to stand or sit. And when invited to, 'make yourself at home', you perch uncomfortably on the edge of an upright chair.

Some houses are chaotic, their owners never able to find what they're looking for. Some have an obviously artistic or high-brow feel to them. Some feel homely and cosy whilst others feel postively hostile – cold, dark and brooding. There there are those which each successive owner occupies for a good twenty or thirty years, growing and establishing a whole new generation in them, whereas an almost identical house in the same street might, for some inexplicable reason, change hands as often as every couple of years or so.

Certainly it is true that houses will reflect their inhabitants, which will, of course, depend a great deal on the occupant's style and taste, not to mention their pocket. Moreover, bricks and mortar, it has been suggested, are able to absorb the atmosphere that people create within their walls – happiness, sadness, avariciousness, malice – and these vibrations may be retained within that residence long, long after its occupants have moved away. These, of course, are the vibrations that sensitive prospective buyers or tenants are likely to pick up.

And isn't it interesting to note how houses seem to attract similar types of people? Perhaps, it might be argued, that's something to do with income brackets – people in the same income band can afford the same type of house. Possibly that is so, but there's more to it than that.

Indeed, there is a good deal more to the character of a house than the vagaries of its occupants, something that is hinted at when every so often one hears people bemoaning their fate: 'Ever since we moved into this house, nothing seems to have gone right!' Or, more positively, others might say, 'Moving was the best thing we ever did. I think our new house has brought us luck!'

Could there be such a thing, then, as a lucky or unlucky house? Or a happy/unhappy, friendly/hostile, warm/cold one. And could it be that people really do find a particular affinity to certain houses, feel immediately comfortable, more at ease in some locations than in others ?

A numerologist would say yes. The answer, they explain, lies in the compatible vibrations between the house and its occupant. Though to state categorically that one house is luckier than another is not quite right. Each house, like each number, has its positive and negative sides. What matters, however, is that the vibratory influence of the house should match that of it's inhabitant. If the two are in harmony, the individual will feel at peace, will flourish and even prosper. If there is an obvious clash, however, the individual may feel hindered, blocked, ill at ease, physically or psychologically unable to progress.

Determining the character of your house and what sort of vibration it is putting out is just a simple process of analysing its number, adding up any multiples until reduced to a single digit. Whether that house is compatible with you, how it will influence your life and how you are likely to react whilst living there, will very much depend on your own date of birth. If the two numbers are in harmony with each other, the situation will be beneficial to you and you will, in all probability thrive in that location. If, however, the two digits are discordant you may feel uneasy there or even, in extreme cases, feel that events in your life are taking a downward turn.

The first step, then, is to analyse the actual number of your house. If you live in a house that's numbered 1 to 9 simply refer to that number in the table of houses below. If yours is a multiple, 32 let's say, add the digits together, $3+2 = 5$, then look up the description for number 5. Any larger number can be reduced in exactly the same way as, for example 296 becomes $2+9+6 = 17 = 1+7 = 8$.

If you live in an apartment within a block of flats, then the number of the block itself must be added to your flat number and reduced to a single digit in the same way.

## EXAMPLE

Flat 9, 25, Acacia Avenue, Manchester
9+2+5 = 16

Total 1+6 = 7

In fact, a block of flats presents a good deal of interest to a numerologist because the number of a particular apartment may in itself be incompatible with the street number of the block. If there is a mis-match in the vibrations, it is possible that petty frustrations or irritations may dog the inhabitants unfortunate enough to reside in that flat. Perhaps this is the one apartment in the whole place where the heating is always going wrong, or the loo keeps getting blocked, where for no apparent reason the television is constantly on the blink, or it has a faster turn-over of occupants than any of the others.

If you live in a flat, check the table of harmonies and oppositions on p. 86 to see if your number vibrates harmoniously or if it is discordant with the actual number of the block of flats itself – this might well explain those nagging domestic problems that seem to be always happening to YOU and never to your neighbour!

Of course, some houses don't have a number at all but are known instead by a name. 'Rose Cottage', so the Royal Mail tells us, is about the most popular name for a house in Britain. To find the vibrational character of 'Rose Cottage', or of 'Buckingham Palace' for that matter, or even of 'The Rover's Return', simply work out the numerical equivalent as you would for a person's name.

**EXAMPLE**

$$R\ O\ S\ E \qquad\qquad C\ O\ T\ T\ A\ G\ E$$
$$9+6+1+5 \qquad\quad 3+6+2+2+1+7+5$$
$$2+1 = 3 \qquad\qquad 2+6 = 8$$
$$3+8 = 11$$

Total $1+1 = 2$

So the character of 'Rose Cottage' may be described by its numerical value of 2.

**EXAMPLE**

$$B\ U\ C\ K\ I\ N\ G\ H\ A\ M \qquad\qquad P\ A\ L\ A\ C\ E$$
$$2+3+3+2+9+5+7+8+1+4 \qquad 7+1+3+1+3+5$$
$$4+4 = 8 \qquad\qquad\qquad 2+0 = 2$$
$$8+2 = 10$$

Total $1+0 = 1$

$$T\ H\ E \qquad\qquad R\ O\ V\ E\ R\ S \qquad\qquad R\ E\ T\ U\ R\ N$$
$$2+8+5 \qquad\quad 9+6+4+5+9+1 \qquad 9+5+2+3+9+5$$
$$1+5 = 6 \qquad\quad 3+4 = 7 \qquad\qquad 3+3 = 6$$
$$6+7+6 = 19$$

Total $1+9 = 1$

How interesting that two institutions, so very different from each other, but each in its own way dear to the nation, should share the same numerical value!

Once you have worked out the number of your residence you need to match that to the day of your birth. If you were born on the 21st of the month your vibrational number would be $2+1 = 3$. And of course it's also 3 if you were born on the 3rd, on the 12th, and on the 30th of the month too. Now check your two numbers against each other in the House-Personal Compatibility Table on p. 86. These vibrational influences apply specifically to a property or residence and should not be used for the purpose of working out compatibility between people.

Of course, this table of affinities is simply a guide and it should be remembered that each number has a positive as well as a negative side to it so that the character of a house will not be all good or all bad. The important thing is to recognise and try to live up to the nature and challenge of, firstly, your own Destiny and Expression numbers and, secondly, to the nature and challenge presented by your environment as expressed by the number of the house in which you live.

If, having tried, you still feel at odds with the vibrational influence of your house in that whatever you do you still feel unsettled, unhappy, blocked, uneasy or whatever, you can take comfort in the fact that, numerically-speaking, there is an easy way out. Short of putting the property on the market again, it is possible to change the negative vibration of a house into a more favourable one simply by changing its numerical value.

So, if you were born on the 22nd (=4) and you're finding it tough living at No. 12 (=3) think about giving your house a name – the numerical equivalent of which, of course, should equal a number compatible with your own.

**EXAMPLE**

$$\begin{array}{lll} \text{T H E} & \text{L A U R E L S} & \\ 2+8+5 & 3+1+3+9+5+3+1 & \\ 1+5 & 2+5 & \\ 6 \quad + & 7 & = 13 \end{array}$$

Total $1+3 = 4$

So 'The Laurels' has a value of 4, which is great because it will have a strong affinity with your own. However, this value has to be added to the existing number of the house which, in this case, is 3 giving a total of 7. Again, this number is fine because it, too, is compatible with your own personal number. Now all you have to do is apply to your local council, who will inform the Royal Mail, arrange for a name-plate to be made, get your letter-heads re-printed and then just bask in your house's reformed character!

## HOUSE-PERSONAL COMPATIBILITY TABLE

| *BIRTH DAY* | *COMPATIBLE HOUSE NUMBERS* | *DISCORDANT HOUSE NUMBERS* |
|---|---|---|
| 1st and all numbers adding to one: 10th, 19th, 28th | All numbers adding to 1 to 2, to 4, and to 7 | All numbers adding to 6 |
| 2nd and all numbers adding to two: 11th, 20th, 29th | All numbers adding to 1, to 2, to 6 and to 8 | All numbers adding to 5 |
| 3rd and all numbers adding to three: 12th, 21st, 30th | All numbers adding to 1, to 3, to 5, to 6, to 7 and to 9 | All numbers adding to 4 |
| 4th and all numbers adding to four: 13th, 22nd, 31st | All numbers adding to 1, to 2, to 4 and to 7 | All numbers adding to 3, to 5 and to 9 |

| BIRTH DAY | COMPATIBLE HOUSE NUMBERS | DISCORDANT HOUSE NUMBERS |
|---|---|---|
| 5th and all numbers adding to five: 14th, and 23rd | All numbers adding to 1, to 3, to 5, to 7, to 8 and to 9 | All numbers adding to 2, to 4 and to 6 |
| 6th and all numbers adding to six: 15th and 24th | All numbers adding to 3, to 6 and to 9 | All numbers adding to 1, to 5, to 7 and to 8 |
| 7th and all numbers adding to seven: 16th and 25th | All numbers adding to 1, to 2, to 4 and to 7 | All numbers adding to 6, to 8 and to 9 |
| 8th and all numbers adding to eight: 17th and 26th | All numbers adding to 1, to 3 and to 8 | All numbers adding to 7 |
| 9th and all numbers adding to nine: 18th and 27th | All numbers adding to 3, to 6 and to 9 | All numbers adding to 4 and to 7 |

## CHARACTER GUIDE TO YOUR HOUSE

### NUMBER 1

No. 1 houses, and all those adding up to 1, may be characterised as lively and dynamic. These are busy, bustling households, full of life and activity. In line with this general bustle, No. 1 houses very often have two entrances, thus augmenting the comings and goings.

Because of the dominant and active nature of this number, occupants of No. 1 houses will be sporty and energetic. So in this home there will be lots of sports equipment lying around. ONE has also an association with creativity, a sense of originality, and because of this there is likely to be evidence throughout of creative projects that have been undertaken. As well as the physical movement there is plenty of mental activity, and the residents here are likely to enjoy intellectual pursuits. Perhaps they play quizz and word games, possibly they indulge in literary pleasures, and there are bound to be one or two computers for the young masterminds in the family. Occupants of No. 1 love travelling and, like all travellers, these people will return with armfulls of memories and souvenirs with which to adorn their nests and which will be constant reminders of their adventures – and of even greater adventures in more distant horizons as yet to be conquered and explored. All in all, No. 1 may be described as a fairly cosmopolitan house.

## NUMBER 2

In contast to the active nature of the No. 1 house, a No. 2 house has a far quieter and more passive feel. There is a definite aura of peacefulness here and its inhabitants will strive to achieve domestic harmony and tranquility. Very often there is a predominantly feminine influence in a No. 2 residence, with evidence of heightened sensitivity all round.

Much attention will be given to detail, although this is often at the expense of the larger, more important and sometimes structural maintainance jobs that need to be routinely carried out. As a consequence, there is a certain ambiguity about this house – on the one hand there is a sense of deterioration yet, on the other, there will be everywhere dotted about strong focal points which have been lavished with a good deal of love and care.

And this ambiguity, this duality which is so much a part of the number TWO nature, can filter through and have a profound effect on the inhabitants. People living here who are not in harmony with its vibrations may especially feel uneasy and find themselves developing obsessional tendencies. In fact, this number is not considered a particularly lucky one and has been associated with ill-heath, especially with certain nervous disorders and mental instability. In some cases, the No. 2 household has been linked with personality complexes, with nervous breakdowns and, in even more severe cases, with psychiatric problems such as schizophrenia.

People who are in harmony with this number, however, will find living here conducive to contemplation, to the growth of deep, inner wisdom and to the development of their spiritual or psychic potential.

## NUMBER 3

The No. 3 house is characterised by its care-free, easy-going atmosphere. Look around and everywhere will be found evidence of a love and appreciation of creativity and art. This home will be filled with many original touches, furnished with flair and decorated with a strong sense of imagination and individuality.

Occupants of No. 3 houses are noted for their wide diversity of interests. New subjects, new ideas, new inventions, new hobbies are a constant source of fascination and half-finished projects will be evident throughout the house – started with great excitement and then left in mid-air as the enthusiasm has worn off.

Activity is a keyword to this lively and colourful home, which sees a constant stream of visitors through its doors. This is a place of mental expansion, of learning and developing one's talents. If the occupants are prepared to take on this challenge, to make full use of their creative instincts, their artistic talents and their

inspirational ideas, they will be rewarded with fulfillment and success.

Indeed, for those who are in harmony with its
vibrations, this is a place of happiness and good cheer.
There will not be a serious sense of want, even if
perhaps money is at times a little tight, for THREE is the
number of abundance and of good fortune.

But for those whose personal number does not
resonate harmoniously with THREE, or who feel unable
to express themselves creatively or imaginatively or,
more importantly, who perhaps take a negative attitude
to life, the picture can be quite the reverse. For these,
unable to meet the challenge for self-expansion that is
demanded by this number, residing here may prove
neither happy nor lucky for them.

## NUMBER 4

Number FOUR is a solid, reliable, hard-working type of
household. An air of stability pervades and throughout
there is a feeling of orderliness, of organization and
regularity.

Here, conservative and traditional values are main-
tained. Roles are likely to be stereotyped and there will
be a strong adherence to rules and regulations. The
work ethic is nowhere more evident than at this address
where discipline and application go hand-in-hand with
duty and responsibility.

Routine is important to the occupants who, in general,
are not considered terribly versatile nor, indeed, great
lovers of change. In fact, they succeed by dint of
constant perseverance at a task, stolidly plodding their
way through to its completion.

There may not be a conspicuous amount of money in
this house for paying professional experts to carry out
building or installation jobs so the onus is likely to fall
upon its inhabitants to do the work themselves.

Fortunately, occupants of No. 4 are hard-working enough to willingly take on the projects but unfortunately, enthusiastic as they might be, they often lack technical expertise and creative flair so that household repairs may end up looking somewhat amateurish.

Indeed, unlike its neighbouring number 3, this house is not famed for its imagination nor, come to that, for its originality and the style of its interior may not be to everyone's taste. Having said that, what this house lacks in creative æsthetics, it more than makes up for in constructive practicality and in the sound and solid basis it provides upon which its inhabitants can build a stable and solid family environment.

## NUMBER 5

No. 5 is typified by lots of comings and goings. Perhaps it is best described as a typical batchelor pad, a pied-a-terre rather than a traditional family home. Somewhere to pass through perhaps but, because of its lack of a stable sense of permanence, it does not inspire you necessarily to see it as a place in which to put down roots and bring up children.

Generally colourful and bright this is, in many instances, a showy type of residence, keeping itself tidy by virtue of the fact that its inhabitants are often away. There is a restless feel to this house and strangely enough No. 5 seems to attract people who tend to be on the move a great deal – commercial travellers, perhaps, or people in the media whose job entails a good deal of travelling around.

That same restlessness means that its occupants hate routine just as much in their home as in their work. Consequently, they like to experiment with different colour-schemes, they move the furniture around, swap items from one room to another so that you may visit this house one week and, on returning the next, find yourself in such unfamiliar surroundings that you think you've gone to the wrong address altogether!

Light and space are often features of this house, created by lots of picture windows and an open-plan effect. But always there is a sensual character to No. 5: rich wines and sweet-meats to interest the palate, deep inviting sofas in which to lose oneself and mirrors everywhere – particularly in the bedroom!

As well as sensuality, there is often an accompanying 'avant guard' or progressive element, with gadgets of all descriptions lying around, and telephones in nearly every room, reflecting the love of communciations that is so much part, not only of the residents, but also of the general Mercurial nature that describes the No. 5 dwelling. It is because of this Mercurial character that No. 5, and any other reducing to 5, does so well as commercial premises.

## NUMBER 6

No. 6 characterises the home. This number is synonomous with domesticity and family life.

Nowhere in the street is the sense of family unity, of domestic togetherness, of hearth and home, more in evidence than at this house. As soon as you walk in through the door you can sense the warm and homely atmosphere, get a feel of the lively, lived-in place, filled with light, noise, laughter and the bustle of domestic confusion.

Children are at the very centre of this home, their toys scattered around, their pictures displayed on the walls, their pets curled up in front of the fire.

Here will be found a blend of the practical with the creative so that there will be evidence of many artistic or handicraft projects everywhere. Perhaps cloths that have been prettily hand embroidered will be draped over tables, tapestries lovingly stitched by the lady of the house will add colour to a dark corner of the room, furniture bought for a song and cleverly reupholstered will take pride of place, flowers fresh from the garden and beautifully arranged in bowls will give out their fragrance – a testiment to the green-fingers of its occupants.

No. 6 encapsulates all that is creative, the love and nurturing of children and family, the spirit of beauty and harmony, and the very heart of the home.

## NUMBER 7

There is something rather impersonal about the No. 7 house. Even its occupants, people who like to keep themselves to themselves, are considered aloof and thus manage to create an air of secrecy or of mystery. They are not in general social types, and, indeed, in many cases neighbours barely know who they are at all. Perhaps one reason for this is that, apart from No. 5, there seems to be a faster turnover of residents at this address than at any other in the road.

From the outside, No. 7 houses can appear somewhat neglected, even a little rundown. There can be a look of faded glory about them, a sense of past grandure now slightly decayed, and yet coupled to that is an implicit feeling that in the right hands their former elegance and beauty could so easily be restored.

Inside, the same sense of elegance, albeit in decline, is also in evidence throughout, matched by obvious attempts at creating a certain stylish interior – although all too often this is achieved at the expense of comfort. Quality rather than quantity being the catchphrase of the number SEVEN, this house is likely to be sparsely furnished, thus adding to its feel of cool detachment.

No. 7 houses generate a quiet and peaceful atmosphere which is conducive to work of an intellectual nature, to study or to inner contemplation rather than to the noisy traffic and hurley-burley of family life. They do especially well as churches, libraries or academic institutions.

## NUMBER 8

The number EIGHT is associated with material security and success, and thus houses with this number on the door, or those adding up to an 8, will reflect an air of prosperity.

The prevailing atmosphere is that of material comfort. Its inhabitants are invariably ambitious, industrious and successful in their work. Often, they are business people and achievement-motivated so they are prepared to work long hours in order to climb the ladder and arrive at their goal. And their efforts are certainly rewarded in material terms.

The long hours that residents of this number put into their jobs or professions means that they are out a lot during the day and thus not available to do many of the every-day routine domestic tasks that are essential to the maintainance and good running of a house. Also, as they earn a good salary, due to all their hard work, they have enough money to buy labour-saving devices and pay others to carry out the jobs that they haven't the time to do for themselves.

Consequently, there is a feeling of affluence around this house, conspicuous consumption, material comforts and, often too, the latest gadgets will be very much in evidence. But what may also be apparent is that the occupants of No. 8 are so busy acquiring their wealth and material possessions that they have little time left in which to establish a warm and loving home-life.

So, residents whose personal number resonates harmoniously with 8 and who are prepared to work hard to achieve both material stability together with emotional fulfillment will be well rewarded during their stay in this house. Those, however, who do not feel an affinity towards this address or who are unable to meet these challenges could well experience financial and emotional set-backs here.

## NUMBER 9

No. 9 houses are very busy places. There is likely to be masses of activity going on here with a constant stream of people passing through. Yet, though there may be lots of irons in the fire, underlying it all will be a general feeling that not a lot is accomplished and that progress in any direction is slow.

Residents of No. 9 houses, or of those adding up to 9, are full of ambitions and good ideas, forever making plans for the future. A good deal of this, however, may be put down to pure day-dreaming because these good intentions are all too often left on the drawing-board or hanging in mid-air. The ideas are there, all right, but the practical application or implementation of them can be sadly lacking in this household.

One of the biggest problems in this respect is that money can be a little tight and there simply isn't enough to cover all those essential little household tasks, let alone stretch to achieving all the dreams and longings of its inhabitants. Sometimes the difficulties lie in the fact that No. 9 occupants are more idealistic than materialistic and simply don't go in for highly-paid occupations. Alternatively, the fact that many are neither practical nor materialistic may suggest that they are unable to manage their finances successfully.

All in all, it is perhaps advisable for these residents to leave their hopes and dreams bubbling away on a back-burner until family demands that drain the purse have diminished and there is time and opportunity to allow their ambitions to materialise.

The prevailing atmosphere in the 9 household is one

of creativity with, for many, a somewhat cosmopolitan feel. As NINE symbolises a global outlook, this house is likely to have a good aspect with plenty of windows that let in light and allow its inhabitants a good vantage point from which to observe the world around them, to contemplate philosophy and the universal truths of life.

## Family Matters Series

A-Z of Childhood Illnesses
  0 7063 6969 6
Anniversary Celebrations
  0 7063 6636 0
Aromatherapy 0 7063 6959 9
Baby's First Year 0 7063 6778 2
Baby's Names 0 7063 6542 9
Baby's Names and Star Signs
  0 7063 6801 0
Barbecue Tips 0 7063 6893 2
Card & Conjuring Tricks
  0 7063 6811 8
Card Games 0 7063 6635 2
Card Games for One 0 7063 6747 2
Card Games for Two 0 7063 6907 6
Catering for a Wedding
  0 7063 6953 X
Charades and Party Games
  0 7063 6637 9
Children's Party Games
  0 7063 6611 5
Christmas Planner 0 7063 6949 1
Common Ailments Cured Naturally
  0 7063 6895 9
Does it Freeze? 0 7063 6960 2
Dreams and Their Meanings
  0 7063 6802 9
Early Learning Games
  0 7063 6771 5

First Time Father 0 7063 6952 1
Handwriting Secrets Revealed
  0 7063 6841 X
How to be a Bridesmaid
  0 7063 7003 1
How to be the Best Man
  0 7063 6748 0
Lovers' Horoscopes 0 7063 6951 3
Microwave Tips & Timings
  0 7063 6812 6
Modern Etiquette 0 7063 6641 7
Naming Baby 0 7063 5854 6
Palmistry 0 7063 6894 0
Preparing for Baby 0 7063 6883 5
Pressure Cooker Tips & Timings
  0 7063 6908 4
Successful Children's Parties
  0 7063 6843 6
Tracing Your Family Tree
  0 7063 6947 5
Travel Games 0 7063 6643 3
Vegetarian Cooking Made Easy
  0 7063 6941 6
Wedding Etiquette 0 7063 6868 1
Wedding Planner, The
  0 7063 6867 3
Wedding Speeches and Toasts
  0 7063 6642 5